Among the
SIOUX
of Dakota

T0272857

Among the
SIOUX
of Dakota

*Eighteen Months' Experience
as an Indian Agent
1869–70*

D. C. Poole

With an introduction by Raymond J. DeMallie

MINNESOTA HISTORICAL SOCIETY PRESS

St. Paul • 1988

2004 reprint of 1988 edition

Minnesota Historical Society Press, St. Paul 55101

Originally published as *Among the Sioux of Dakota: Eighteen Months Experience as an Indian Agent*, copyright 1881 by D. Van Nostrand.

New material copyright 1988 by the Minnesota Historical Society

International Standard Book Number 0-87351-210-3
Manufactured in the United States of America

10 9 8 7 6 5 4 3 2 1

Library of Congress Cataloging-in-Publication Data

Poole, D. C. (DeWitt Clinton), 1828–1917.
    Among the Sioux of Dakota : eighteen months' experience as an
Indian agent, 1869–70 / D.C. Poole ; with an introduction by
Raymond J. DeMallie.
        p.   cm.
    Reprint. Originally published: New York : Van Nostrand, 1881.
    Includes index.
    ISBN 0-87351-210-3
    1. Dakota Indians – Government relations. 2. Poole, D. C. (DeWitt
Clinton), 1828–1917. 3. Indian agents – United States – Biography.
4. Indians of North America – Government relations – 1869–1934.
I. Title.
E99.D1P8 1988
978.3'00497 – dc19   87-28158
                                                                CIP

CONTENTS

CHAPTER XXXIII.

CHAPTER XXXIV.

CHAPTER XXXV.

CHAPTER XXXVI.

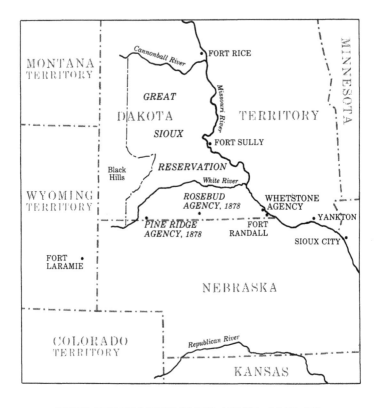

THE NORTHERN PLAINS, 1869-70

INTRODUCTION
TO THE REPRINT EDITION

FRONTIER Indian agents were the representatives of the federal government's program to pacify and bring to "civilization" the native peoples of the West. As DeWitt Clinton Poole wrote in *Among the Sioux of Dakota: Eighteen Months Experience As An Indian Agent*, they were called on to serve "without the boundaries of civilization, isolated from the associations and comforts of a home," public scapegoats for any Indian troubles that might arise, and believed to be dishonest by the very fact of their association with Indians. With the dry wit that permeates his reminiscence, Poole commented of the Indian agent that "his lines are not cast in pleasant places" (p. 227).

While the agents' daily, bureaucratic correspondence has preserved a massive archival record of their official activities, few wrote anything for publication to explicate or justify their service. Per-

haps their silence has contributed to the general
sentiment of their culpability. But if Indian agents
tended to leave their careers unmemorialized, military officers did not. The last decades of the nine-
teenth century saw an explosion in the publication
of personal memoirs of military service in the Civil
War and frontier Indian wars. Poole's book fits into
this literary genre, and—like Custer's *My Life on
the Plains* (1874) and Dodge's *Our Wild Indians*
(1882)—it is tinged with the spirit of reform, following the army's consistent faith that military men
were better suited to deal with the "Indian problem" than civilians.[1]

Poole's *Among the Sioux of Dakota* is important
because it fleshes out the social context of the
author's experience as agent, depicting the dynam-
ics of daily life in a way that escapes record in his
official correspondence. It is therefore a valuable
document for understanding what life was like at
the Sioux agencies in the early years of the Great
Sioux Reservation, established by treaty in 1868.
Moreover, in conjunction with Poole's official correspondence (now in the National Archives), this
book is the only source for writing the history of
the short-lived Whetstone Agency, intended to

1. George A. Custer, *My Life on the Plains: Or, Personal Ex-
periences with the Indians* (New York: Sheldon & Co., 1874);
Richard Irving Dodge, *Our Wild Indians: Thirty-Three Years'
Personal Experience among the Red Men of the Great West*
(Hartford, Conn.: A. D. Worthington and Company, 1882).

have been the permanent home of the Oglala and Brule Sioux (Lakotas).[2] Poole's narrative also provides a lengthy account of the 1870 Sioux delegation to Washington, D.C., an important historical milestone, for it was on this trip – the first visit of Spotted Tail and Red Cloud to the capital – that the the chiefs received government sanction to have their agencies moved from the Missouri River westward to the White River. There, eight years later, after many false starts and the intervening Sioux War of 1876, the permanent agency headquarters of Rosebud (for the Brules) and Pine Ridge (for the Oglalas) were at last established.

Published in 1881, Poole's book does not seem to have attracted much contemporary attention, although it was praised by one military reviewer as "a most entertaining as well as instructive little

2. On Poole's correspondence, see note 8, below. "Sioux" is the usual English term for those people who call themselves *Dakota* and *Lakota*, the former being the self-designation of those groups living mostly east of the Missouri River in the mid-nineteenth century (the Santees, Yanktons, and Yanktonais), and the latter of those living mostly west of the Missouri (the Tetons). The Oglalas and Brules are the southernmost of the Teton groups. The word "Sioux" comes originally from the Chippewa name for these people, *na·towe·ssiwak*, meaning "enemies." See Ives Goddard, "The Study of Native North American Ethnonymy," in Elisabeth Tooker, ed., *Naming Systems*, 1980 Proceedings of the American Ethnological Society (Washington, D.C.: The Society, 1984), 105.

work on 'Our Indian Question.' "[3] It has been cited only infrequently in the historical literature. The print run must have been quite small, as it is today a scarce volume, lacking even from major library collections. This reprint will bring the book and its author long overdue attention, but to appreciate Poole's narrative, whose tone will strike the modern reader as paternalistic and even racist, it is necessary to understand it in the context of its time.

DeWitt Clinton Poole was born on September 28, 1828, in the Mohawk Valley of New York.[4] As a young man he received training in business, and he moved west to Madison, Wisconsin, in 1854. With the outbreak of the Civil War, he joined the Wisconsin Volunteers in April 1861 as first lieutenant of Company K. After the expiration of his term of enlistment that August, he joined the Twelfth Wisconsin Regiment as lieutenant colonel. Two years later, in the fall of 1863, he was relieved from active duty and appointed lieutenant colonel in the Veter-

3. Review by "T. W." in *Journal of the Military Service Institution of the United States* 3 (1882): 140.

4. Information about Poole's life has been taken from a biography written by his son, John Hudson Poole, *American Cavalcade: A Memoir on the Life and Family of DeWitt Clinton Poole* (Pasadena, California: privately printed, 1939), and from his official military file in the National Archives and Records Service (NARS, Record Group 94, 3890 ACP 1877).

an Reserve Corps, taking a position as instructor at Cliffburn Barracks, D.C. He returned to active duty the next year with the Army of Virginia, serving as provost marshal first in Washington, D.C., then in Scranton, Pennsylvania. In 1865 he was detailed to Atlanta to serve under General O. O. Howard in the Freedman's Bureau. He resigned in the spring of 1866, returning to Madison, but following the army reorganization of 1867, he was commissioned a captain and reassigned to duty in Atlanta. It was there, in the spring of 1869 – as he related in his book – that he received the order detailing him to duty as Indian agent at Whetstone Agency, Dakota Territory (p. 9). Poole wrote, "Usually the Indian agent comes in contact with his duties perfectly unprepared by experience" (p. 228); his own case was no exception.

The historical circumstances that brought Captain Poole to Whetstone Agency were complex and of long duration.[5] The government had first faced

5. The most important studies of Brule and Oglala Sioux history during the 1850s and 1860s are two volumes by George E. Hyde, *Red Cloud's Folk: A History of the Oglala Sioux Indians* (Norman: University of Oklahoma Press, 1937; rev. ed., 1957) and *Spotted Tail's Folk: A History of the Brulé Sioux* (Norman: University of Oklahoma Press, 1961); and James C. Olson, *Red Cloud and the Sioux Problem* (Lincoln: University of Nebraska Press, 1965). For an understanding of the military perspective, see the two volumes by Robert M. Utley, *Fron-*

the issue of growing competition between the Western Sioux and United States citizens in 1851 at the great multitribal treaty council staged at Horse Creek, near Fort Laramie, which had been established two years earlier to provide some U.S. military presence on the Overland Trail. At that council, responding to the government commissioner's demands, the Sioux present elected a "head chief" who was supposed to represent them in all future dealings with the whites and accept responsibility for monitoring his people's conduct. The unfortunate Brule chief Brave Bear, on whom the honor fell, commented ominously that if he were not a "strong chief," he would soon be lying dead on the prairie. His prophecy came true on Au-

---

tiersmen in Blue: The United States Army and the Indian, 1848-1865 (New York: Macmillan, 1967) and *Frontier Regulars: The United States Army and the Indian, 1866-1890* (New York: Macmillan, 1973). The best survey of governmental policy toward the Indians is Francis Paul Prucha, *The Great Father: The United States Government and the American Indians*, 2 vol. (Lincoln: University of Nebraska Press, 1984). I have drawn on each of these works in writing this introduction.

For the history of Whetstone Agency, see Richmond L. Clow, "The Whetstone Indian Agency, 1868-1872," *South Dakota History* 7 (1977): 291-308, and John E. Mills, "Historic Sites Archeology in the Fort Randall Reservoir," River Basin Surveys Papers 16, Smithsonian Institution, Bureau of American Ethnology, Bulletin 176, *River Basins Surveys Papers 15-20*, ed. Frank H. H. Roberts (Washington, D.C.: Government Printing Office, 1960), 25-48.

gust 19, 1854, when, unable to persuade a visiting
Minneconjou Sioux who had killed an emigrant's
cow on the Overland Trail to surrender at Fort
Laramie, troops under Lieutenant John L. Grattan
marched to the Brule camp and opened fire with a
howitzer. The chief was killed, but the headstrong
lieutenant and all of his twenty-nine men also paid
with their lives. In November, a Brule war party
attacked the mail coach on its way to Fort
Laramie, killing the two drivers and a passenger,
and making off with a reported $20,000 in the mail
pouches. Other raids occurred during the fall and
resumed in the spring.

Responding to the situation, the army sent
General William S. Harney to squelch the hostilities.[6] He was an officer of considerable experience
with Indians, including witnessing as a lieutenant
with General Henry Atkinson the various treaties
signed in 1825 with the tribes on the upper Missouri. Ordered to make the Sioux feel the wrath of the
government for the Grattan affair, he set out from
Fort Kearney, following the Overland Trail west.
Near Ash Hollow, on Blue Water Creek, he found
a Brule camp under Little Thunder. Surrounding
the village with his more than six hundred troops,

6. For a biographical sketch see Richmond L. Clow, "William
S. Harney," in *Soldiers West: Biographies from the Military
Frontier*, ed. Paul Andrew Hutton (Lincoln: University of
Nebraska Press, 1987), 42–58.

Harney attacked on the morning of September 3, 1855; of the estimated 250 Brules, 86 were killed and some 70 women and children were captured. Marching on to Fort Laramie, the general demanded that the murderers of the mail coach party be turned over for punishment. On September 18 the warriors surrendered, two of them brothers of the deceased Brave Bear and the third, Spotted Tail. The prisoners were sent to Fort Leavenworth for the winter, returned to Fort Kearney in May—having received presidential pardons—and arrived back among their people in September 1856, a year after their surrender. This experience is credited with having convinced Spotted Tail of the necessity of cooperating with the whites and having turned him into an advocate of peace.

While Spotted Tail and his companions were on their way to Fort Leavenworth, Harney took his prisoners from Fort Laramie to the Missouri River, across Sioux country, and established a military fort at the fur-trading post of Fort Pierre. There in March 1856 he convened a council with representatives of all the Sioux on the Missouri and signed with them a treaty of peace, which he intended as the foundation for future governing of their affairs. Each Sioux tribe named a head chief and subordinate chiefs, and it was proposed that a number of "soldiers" be appointed to enforce the chiefs' orders.

At the conclusion of the council, Harney and the

leaders of the Sioux seemed mutually assured that the treaty would end the difficulties between the Indians and whites. Instead, it was only another false start. Harney had no authority to negotiate a treaty with the Sioux, and even though he received backing from President Franklin Pierce, Congress failed to appropriate the funds necessary to carry out the agreement.

During the ensuing decade, relations between the Sioux and the encroaching white settlements continued to worsen. The Minnesota Sioux troubles of 1862 ultimately involved the Western Sioux in the conflict when, in 1864, General Alfred Sully pursued the Santees onto the prairies of eastern Dakota Territory and engaged the Teton Sioux at the Battle of Killdeer Mountain on July 28. To the south, hostilities between the Cheyennes and the whites culminated in the Sand Creek massacre on November 29, 1864, when more than a hundred Cheyenne men, women, and children were slain under a flag of truce by Colonel John B. Chivington's volunteer forces.

At the close of the Civil War, Congress was not anxious to spend more money to fight an Indian war in the West. A formal investigation of the Sand Creek affair faulted the soldiers, not the Indians, and government policy settled on the strategy of seeking peace with the Indians and localizing them on reservations, recommending it as both cheaper and more humane than fighting them. President

Andrew Johnson appointed the first of a series of peace commissions in 1865, which every year through 1868 made summer pilgrimages throughout the plains to sign treaties with the various tribes.

Even as the peace commissions were doing their work, the army was fighting Indians. The campaigns of General Winfield Scott Hancock in 1867 and of General Philip Sheridan in 1868-69 against the Cheyennes and other tribes of the southern plains kept the region south of the Sioux in constant turmoil. The Bozeman Trail, a short cut from Fort Laramie to the gold fields of Montana, traversed Sioux hunting grounds on the west, and the building of military posts between 1865 and 1867 to guard the trail was no less than a declaration of war against Red Cloud's Oglalas and other Western Sioux and Cheyennes. When, on December 21, 1866, the Sioux lured Colonel William J. Fetterman and a detachment of eighty men out of the beleaguered Fort Philip Kearny and killed them all, the government again responded with offers of peace, rather than mounting a military campaign of the magnitude necessary to crush the Sioux. Finally, the 1868 peace commission signed treaties with the various bands that guaranteed the Sioux possession of their lands in Dakota Territory, closed the posts on the Bozeman Trail, left the area of Wyoming and Montana to the west of the Black Hills as unceded Indian territory, and promised the Sioux the right to hunt buffalo in the Republican River country of Nebraska and Kansas as long as the herds remained.

The 1868 treaty set the context for all future dealings between the Western Sioux and the United States. Ratified by the Senate, it was the final triumph of the government's peace policy as it related to the Sioux. But the peace commission that negotiated the treaty was itself composed of more military men than civilians, and it was dominated by General William T. Sherman. Another of its members was General Harney, to whom—by virtue of his earlier experience—was entrusted the management of the Sioux after the treaty was proclaimed. For Congress, suspicious of the Indian Office, appropriated the monies to the War Department to carry out the terms of the treaty. The new Sioux reservation was established on the model of a military district, called the "Sioux District," and was placed entirely under Harney's control. The commission decided—largely on the grounds of economy—to locate the agency headquarters, designated in the treaty to feed and look after the Sioux, near Fort Randall, on the Missouri River, in the southeastern corner of the reservation. In this manner the Whetstone Agency came into existence in 1868. Recognizing the impracticality of managing all the Sioux from a single agency, Harney established two others farther upriver, at Grand River, near Fort Rice, for the Hunkpapas,

Blackfeet Sioux, and Yanktonais; and at Cheyenne River, near Fort Sully, for the Minneconjous, Sans Arcs, and Two Kettles. Whetstone Agency itself would serve the Brules and Oglalas.[7]

The election of Ulysses S. Grant to the presidency ushered in a period of Indian reform. To break the cycle of dishonest agents conspiring with dishonest contractors to cheat the Indians out of the food and goods legally due them from the government, Grant temporarily turned many of the Indian agencies over to military officers. A congressional act in 1869 reducing the size of the army had resulted in a surplus of military officers; sixty-eight of them were assigned to duty as Indian agents. In April 1869, scarcely a month after his inauguration, Grant created the Board of Indian Commissioners, an independent body of Christian philanthropists who served without pay to advise on Indian policy. The next year, under the board's guidance, the Indian agencies were removed from military control, and the selection of Indian agents was turned over to the church groups that had missionized on the various reservations. It was during this interlude of military control, as the contours of

7. Col. Stanley's letter of August 20, 1869, which Poole printed as an appendix (p. 231–35), presents a convenient overview of the Sioux groups and their locations; it was published in the *Report of the Commissioner of Indian Affairs, Made to the Secretary of the Interior, for the Year 1869* (Washington, D.C.: Government Printing Office, 1870), 330–31.

Grant's peace policy took shape, that Captain Poole
was detailed to duty as an Indian agent.

Testing the peace policy to its limit, General Harney spent lavishly in an attempt to pacify both the
Sioux and the frontier settlers. The purchase and
shipping of food and goods to the Indians brought
prosperity to the region, though Harney paid in
vouchers, rather than cash, running some million
dollars into debt without authorization from any
branch of government. Congress bailed the general out by appropriating the money to pay off the
vouchers. But graft, or ill fortune, or mismanage-
ment had transformed what Harney perceived as
a solid investment into a squandering of public
funds. As Poole related in his book, when he arrived at Whetstone virtually all agency equipment
was unserviceable, and the only buildings were
crude log structures (p. 30). Under these unenvia-
ble circumstances, Poole found himself in the
thankless position of serving as a military officer in
a civilian branch of the government. Worse, he
found himself heir to a situation that–from the Indians' point of view, at least–had been personally
shaped during the preceding fourteen years by another military officer, General Harney, whose policy toward the Sioux had begun with warfare and
developed into a series of promises that he was unable to keep.

With this background, we can turn to Captain

Poole's narrative. I have used his official correspondence and other contemporary sources to supplement his own account, identifying when possible the names of individuals alluded to in the text, as well as dates and places.

When Captain Poole arrived on the Missouri he was completely unacquainted with Indians, and, as he wrote, began by visiting General Harney at Sioux City, Iowa, in hopes of receiving useful advice. Poole presents an unimpressive portrait of Harney, who, fully realizing his inability to deliver the goods he had promised to the Indians, was therefore unable to return among them. Probably he took Harney's advice at face value, when the general said of the Indians, "They are children, sir" (p. 15), for Poole's assessment of the Sioux – born of his frustration at their obdurate lack of interest in farming – was that they exhibited "a childlike interest in the present and small care for the future" (p. 39). With such an attitude, the agent's relationship with the Indians under his charge could only be a paternalistic one.

On his arrival in Yankton, Dakota Territory, Poole found territorial governor John A. Burbank – ex-officio superintendent of Indian affairs – no more helpful than Harney, for the governor had not yet even visited Whetstone Agency (p. 22), and it was not until his arrival at Fort Randall, thirty miles south of the agency by river (eighteen miles by wagon road on the east

side of the Missouri), that the new agent was able
to learn anything substantial about the Indians
who would be under his charge.

The majority of the Sioux assigned to the agency
had no intention of settling at Whetstone, and if
they had, they would not have considered agriculture a potentially honorable activity for men as
long as there was game to hunt. Poole himself appreciated this aspect of Sioux culture, noting that
the men were "not indolent and lazy," but were con-
tempuous of labor that they did not consider the
proper work of men (p. 100). In his book he even
proposed that the Sioux should be given livestock
and taught to become pastoralists as the logical
first step toward the more civilized pursuit of
agriculture. But in his official correspondence as an
Indian Office bureaucrat, he did not question policy
and reported only his efforts to interest the Indians
in farming.[8]

At the agency site near the mouth of Whetstone
Creek, Poole found some 1,500 Indians living in tipi

8. Poole's correspondence as Whetstone agent with Burbank
and with Commissioner of Indian Affairs Ely S. Parker is in
NARS, RG 75, Office of Indian Affairs, and is reproduced on
M234 (Letters Received by the Office of Indian Affairs), rolls
251 (Dakota Superintendency, 1868–70), and 894–96 (Upper
Platte Agency, 1869–70); and M1016 (Dakota Superintendency
Records), rolls 7 and 9 (1869, 1870). Throughout this introduction, I have minimized the number of notes by giving citations
only when referring to or quoting from a specific document.

encampments (p. 33–34). The largest number were of the Oglala Loafer band, under the leadership of Big Mouth. There was also a small Oglala camp under Fire Thunder, and the Brule Corn band had two small camps, under Swift Bear and Standing Elk. These groups had been living near Fort Laramie before the 1868 treaty, the Loafer band having coalesced around the post and incorporated many in-married white men and their mixed-blood children. At Whetstone there were, according to Poole, some seventy-seven white men with Indian wives, and the agent considered them as the Indians' most effective instructors in the ways of civilization. During the previous spring, working with their white in-laws, these Indians had cultivated 450 acres.

To the west of the agency, from thirty to sixty miles distant, the Brule chief Spotted Tail maintained his camp of as many as four hundred lodges, some 2,050 people, including Two Strikes' Brules and a group of Oglalas under Black Bear (p. 34, 51). They had no desire to farm and claimed the right under their treaty to have their agency moved up the White River, away from the Missouri where there was no game and the traffic in illegal alcohol proved disastrous to orderly living.[9]

9. On July 31, 1869, Poole estimated the agency population at 1,650, and Spotted Tail's camp at 1,850. Although he believed these figures to be reasonably correct, he commented: "It is im-

Historical evidence suggests that the Sioux leaders did not fully understand the treaty when they touched the pen to it the previous year. But in Poole's first annual report to the Indian Office in August 1869, he wrote that the chiefs at Whetstone had signed it in good faith, "distinctly remembered" its provisions, recalled the promises made to them by the peace commissioners, and in light of their non-fulfillment asked, "Who can they believe now?"[10] It is abundantly clear, however, that the Sioux had not understood that they were expected to return to the Missouri River, where the buffalo herds necessary to support their way of life no longer were to be found. And the guarantee that they could continue to hunt "on any lands north of North Platte" and on the Republican River, in southwestern Nebraska and northwestern Kansas, "so long as the buffalo may range thereon in such numbers as to justify the chase," was written into Article 11 of the treaty. Yet before a year had passed, government officials forbade the Sioux from hunting in Nebraska and were attempting to locate them all within the confines of the

---

possible to procure the accurate number of Indians at this Agency at present owing to their continual outgoings and incomings" (Poole to Burbank, August 3, 1869, M234, roll 894, D429 1869).

10. Poole to Commissioner of Indian Affairs, August 20, 1869, in *Report of the Commissioner of Indian Affairs . . . 1869*, 316.

reservation—this despite the fact that, as Poole noted in his annual report, there were no buffalo herds at all within the reservation boundaries. Settlement on the reservation, therefore, would force the Indians to rely on the agency for food, clothing, and even material with which to patch their tipis.

When Poole arrived at his station, the treaty annuity goods for the Indians of the agency had not yet been purchased. Some $2,500 worth of goods— about one-fourth of what the Indians were entitled to receive—were diverted from the Upper Missouri Agency supplies for distribution at Whetstone. In his book the agent described the manner of distribution of these meager supplies, and the Indians' dissatisfaction with the quantity (p. 56). Even before the distribution, on July 21, Poole wrote to the commissioner of Indian affairs sending estimates for more blankets, cloth, items of clothing, tools, and other goods to make up the required amount. In early August he learned that Harney had several thousand suits of clothing (coats and pants) in Sioux City, and he requested that a thousand suits be added to his previous order for annuity goods. He wrote again on July 31, on August 20, and yet a fourth time on September 3, pleading for action on his requests. In the last letter he commented, "I am forced to say that I do not expect the Indians upon the Reservation to remain peaceable and quiet this fall and winter unless more goods are forwarded, which they have every right to expect.

When they compare their situation with neighbouring tribes—My Indians are really poor. They have but few blankets. Their tepes are all nearly worn out."[11]

Recognizing its obligation to the Whetstone Indians, the Indian Office authorized the purchase of the additional goods as well as the suits of clothing. However, it was mid-October before they arrived and were distributed. The Sioux were not pleased with the clothing, which did not meet their standards of usefulness, and complained of the lack of blankets and tobacco. Poole asked for eight hundred "pairs" of blankets (woven double-width) and fifty boxes of tobacco; these, too, were approved, but they were not received at the agency until February 1870, together with the balance of the annuity goods (p. 114).

The threat of violence hung constantly over Whetstone Agency. In July 1869 the Oglala camp under Pawnee Killer and Whistler, while hunting on the Republican River, was attacked by the Pawnee scouts serving with Major Eugene A. Carr. Later these Oglalas straggled into the agency, Poole wrote in his letter of September 3, "in a perfectly destitute condition." A group of Sioux women and children, captured by Carr's forces, was imprisoned at Omaha, and at the request of the

11. Poole to Burbank, September 3, 1869 (M1016, roll 7, frames 208–11).

chiefs Poole wrote the military authorities asking their release. The prisoners were sent to Whetstone in August. Relatives of the Sioux killed in the fighting clamored for revenge. A war party went out and returned with five Pawnee scalps. In return, Pawnee horse raiders preyed on the Sioux herds. These events are more fully described in Poole's book than in his official correspondence (p. 58–62).

Early in August, some three hundred Brules under Red Leaf, Blue Horse, and Big Rib arrived from the vicinity of Fort Laramie, where, since the treaty, they were no longer allowed to trade.[12] These Sioux who had not yet settled on the reservation were better clothed and fed than those under Poole's charge (p. 101). If the government did not keep its promise to deliver an adequate supply of annuity goods, the agency chiefs warned, they would not be able to prevent their young men from going to war during the winter.

Exacerbating the tenseness was the influx of whiskey at the agency, the illegal spirits originating with licensed traders living across the Missouri River. On July 31 Poole wrote to Governor Burbank that the river was low enough to be forded easily and that the illicit trade took place after nightfall. Although the agent noted that regular drinking to excess was indulged in by "many of the

12. Poole to Burbank, August 14, 1869 (M234, roll 894, D465).

half-breeds" and only a dozen or so Indians (p. 79), the explosive potential of strong drink in an atmosphere of discontent was unquieting. On September 28, Lieutenant A. E. Woodson, in charge of Indian susbsistence stores at Whetstone, wrote officially to Poole to report that recent disturbances resulting from whiskey drinking had caused the loss of public property – apparently beef cattle – and he requested that troops be called to the agency for protection of lives and property. On October 1, Poole forwarded the lieutenant's letter to the commissioner of Indian affairs, through Governor Burbank's office in Yankton, asking that a full company of infantry and two mountain howitzers be ordered to the agency. The governor supported the request, noting that an Indian outbreak would have a "demoralizing effect" on the territory.[13]

On October 28, before any action was taken on the agent's letter, the tranquility of the agency was broken by the unfortunate shooting of Big Mouth by Spotted Tail in a drunken melee. Poole went to Big Mouth's camp to visit the dying chief, taking with him the agency physician, Dr. James F. Cravens, who had arrived at Whetstone only six

13. Poole to Burbank, July 31, 1869 (M1016, roll 7, frames 125-34); Burbank to Acting Commissioner of Indian Affairs, October 1, 1869, enclosing Poole's letter of the same date and Woodson's letter of September 28 (M234, roll 894, D544).

days earlier. Once again, Poole's book provides much more detail than his official correspondence. Although Poole exonerated Spotted Tail of any wrongdoing–presenting it as a case of self-defense–the situation at the agency was finally drawn to a head, and the agent called for troops from Fort Randall (p. 83–92). Finding everything quiet, they stayed only a day, arresting three men accused of selling whiskey and taking them back to the fort as prisoners. These events did little to slow the introduction of whiskey to the agency, and white men there who were married to Indian women warned Poole that one more drunken brawl would "lead directly to a war upon the whites."[14]

General Philip Sheridan, commander of the Military Division of the Missouri, had proposed a plan in September to build blockhouses at the Whetstone, Cheyenne, and Grand River agencies on the Great Sioux Reservation and garrison them to keep close watch over the Indians. Colonel David S. Stanley, in charge of the Middle District, headquartered at Fort Sully, was ordered to carry out the project, even though he complained that such a move was "impolitic." Major N. E. G. Whistler, at Fort Randall, also believed that placing troops at the agencies would "demoralize the Indians," but as commander of the nearest post to Whetstone he

14. Poole to Burbank, November 5, 1869 (M1016, roll 7, frames 310–18).

was ordered to provide the troops called for. On December 1, Poole submitted an estimate and plan for garrisoning a company of infantry (one hundred men) at the agency. But on December 18 he suggested that only twenty-five men and an officer be detailed to the agency, to be rotated every month to prevent them from establishing "too intimate relations" with the Indians; the smaller number could be more easily accommodated.[15]

A detachment of fourteen men and an officer was sent to Whetstone in December and began construction of the blockhouses. In January 1870 Poole wrote to Governor Burbank, "The arrival of this small detachment of troops has been of great assistance to me in surpressing [sic] in part the traffic in intoxicating liquor by the moral effect of their presence and I am fully convinced their presence is necessary as long as the present mixture of Indians, Whites & Half Breeds remains at this Agency." In his monthly report for February Poole noted that twenty-five men and an officer were stationed at the post at Whetstone Agency, and he repeated his assertion that their presence had largely succeeded in halting the sale of illegal alco-

15. Stanley to Whistler, November 20, 1869 (NARS, RG 393, Fort Randall, Letters Received); Whistler to Stanley, November 12, 1869 (NARS, RG 393, Department of Dakota, Middle District, Letters Received, W20 1869); Poole to Whistler, December 18, 1869 (NARS, RG 393, Fort Randall, Letters Received).

hol. On March 29, Major Whistler, at Fort Randall, reported to his superiors that the blockhouses at Whetstone were completed and requested authority to send artillery to defend them. By May Poole was able to write that the Indians were cooperating with the soldiers: "I am very glad to report that there is very little drunkenness at the Agency, and that the Indians themselves were instrumental in keeping whiskey away from here."[16]

The lessening of problems with alcohol did not, however, effectively reduce the level of tension at the agency. Spotted Tail continually pressed to move the agency to a site on White River, and Poole felt that the best solution would be to establish a subagency there for the Brules, leaving the Oglalas under Swift Bear to farm at Whetstone. The Indians also pressed for permission to go on a buffalo hunt in the Republican River country. Agreeing that they were in real need of the robes which the hunt would provide, Poole urged the commissioner of Indian affairs to allow the hunters to go out with a responsible white man to oversee their movements; otherwise, he repeatedly warned, the young men would simply go off without permission and trouble might result. Although the commissioner supported Poole's recommendation, with the suggestion that a small military

16. Poole to Burbank, January 4, 1870 and May 4, 1870 (M1016, roll 9, frames 174–78, 353–58).

detachment accompany the hunting party, the proposition was rejected by Secretary of War William W. Belknap on the grounds that the situation on the Kansas border was "too sensitive"; the settlements there were too weak to defend themselves; the buffalo were scarce; and, in any case, the Indians should be home cultivating the soil on their reservation. "It may be added to these reasons," the secretary wrote, "that the Department is unwilling to expose the small military force which alone can be spared to accompany these Indians to the contingency of being massacred by overwhelming numbers, should possible difficulties arise."[17] Clearly, from the War Department's perspective, peace with the Sioux had been only tenuously established.

Yet another disturbing element was the report that began to circulate in February that an exploring expedition was outfitting at Cheyenne, Wyoming, to prospect for gold in the Bighorn Mountains of northern Wyoming, in unceded Indian country, and that in fact the expedition might head for the Black Hills, within the reservation limits. Poole noted in March that newspaper accounts even went so far as to claim that the miners would be accompanied by three hundred U.S. troops. Rumors flew among the Indians. Roman Nose

17. Secretary Belknap to Secretary of the Interior, March 31, 1870 (M234, roll 896, W806, frames 554-55).

brought his camp of Minneconjous to Whetstone from the Powder River country, saying that he had come to trade. He reported that the Sioux warriors were moving toward the Union Pacific Railroad, and that the mining expedition from Cheyenne would meet with opposition all the way. Poole commented, "I am well convinced all the Sioux Indians are watching the movements of this expedition, and should it move as announced, will surely inaugurate an Indian war in that part of the country."[18] In March General Christopher C. Augur, commanding the Department of the Platte from headquarters at Omaha, visited Cheyenne to investigate the situation, eventually putting a stop to the expedition.

For their part, the Indians at Whetstone Agency were doing all in their power to maintain the peace. On March 7, 1870, abiding by the letter of the treaty, the camp soldiers of one of the bands of agency Indians confiscated seven horses from a war party of Yanktons and Lower Brules, who had stolen them from whites living near the Pawnee reservation. These were turned over to the commanding officer at Fort Randall and were eventually returned to their owners. In April the camp soldiers punished two men who went on a raid to the

18. Poole to Burbank, March 4, 1869 (M234, roll 895, D966), and Poole to Burbank, May 4, 1870 (M1016, roll 9, frames 353–58).

south by destroying their families' tipis at the agency; this was the accepted penalty for men who disobeyed the orders of the chiefs and the camp council. Although Spotted Tail and the other chiefs were able to control hostilities against whites, they were unable to prevent war parties from harassing the Pawnees, as the undated letter of spring 1870 from Pawnee agent Jacob M. Troth to Poole testifies (p. 131–32).

In the fall of 1869, perhaps attempting to forestall the outbreak of warfare between the Sioux and the whites that seemed at that time to be nearly inevitable, Spotted Tail and Swift Bear requested agent Poole to write to Washington to ask permission for them to visit their Great Father, each in company of one of the head soldiers of his band. The idea was the Indians' own, and both the agent and Governor Burbank supported it enthusiastically. The next April, Red Cloud, too, asked to visit Washington, conveying his request through the commanding officer at Fort Fetterman. On May 3 the matter was discussed by the cabinet, where the decision was made to invite the Oglala and Brule chiefs; that same day the commissioner of Indian affairs wrote to Poole instructing the agent to start at once for Washington, bringing Spotted Tail and Swift Bear, each with a head soldier, together with an interpreter. The letter arrived May 20 in Yankton, and the governor's office forwarded it by special messenger to Whetstone.

Oddly, Poole recounted in his book that Spotted Tail refused for four days to comply with the request, even suggesting that the Great Father should meet the delegation halfway. Since Poole did not mention in the book that the Indians had been the first to propose the trip, he made no suggestion of what might have caused the change of attitude. In the end the agent persuaded them, however; Spotted Tail selected Fast Bear to represent the Brule warriors, and Swift Bear selected Yellow Hair, head soldier of Fire Thunder's camp, to represent the Oglalas. Poole selected Charles E. Gueru to accompany the delegation as interpreter (p. 134–37).

The Whetstone delegation set off on May 17, and Poole wrote a graphic account of their adventures on the trip east (p. 140–53). At Pittsburgh they met Felix R. Brunot, president of the Board of Indian Commissioners (whose name Poole misspelled, and whom he offhandedly referred to as a member of the "Peace Commission"). The Indians failed to appreciate Brunot's position and paid him little attention—possibly taking their cue from Captain Poole. Given the Board's opposition to military officers as Indian agents, the meeting may not have been cordial.

Finally, on May 23, the delegation reached Washington and lodged near the Capitol at the Washington House on Pennsylvania Avenue, a hotel that frequently hosted Indian delegations. That evening the members went for a walk and their presence did not escape the press: "They were dressed in their native costume—buckskin legging[s] and moccasons, elaborately worked with beads. Around their bodies they wore a blanket, with a white stripe diagonally across it. Strapped about their waist, but out of view, each savage carried his six-shooter, and in his hand his pipe."[19] Only after arriving in Washington were the Whetstone Indians told that Red Cloud was also on his way; according to the newspaper, the delegates were skeptical of the news, and suspected that the white people were deceiving them.

On May 25, surrounded by crowds of onlookers, Poole and the delegation made their way to the cars that would take them to the Indian Office.[20] Arriving there in the morning, they were informed that Commissioner of Indian Affairs Ely S. Parker had gone to the War Department. The delegation immediately left and returned in the afternoon, when they had a short interview with the commissioner, more ceremony than substance, as described by Poole (p. 159–60).

During subsequent days, the agent was instructed to keep the Indians busy seeing the sights of

19. "Arrival of Distinguished Scalp-Hunters—Habits of the Gentle Savage," *New York Herald*, May 25, 1870, p. 3.
20. "Disadvantages of Civilization," *New York Herald*, May 26, 1870, p. 10.

Washington, although they proved to be unen-
thusiastic tourists. Poole recorded few details of
their adventures. Apparently his account of these
events, based undoubtedly on his diary as well as
memory, also drew on a collection of newspaper
clippings, for he refutes the claim that on visiting
Mount Vernon, the Indians stuck their hands
through the iron grating of Washington's tomb to
shake hands with the first Great Father (p. 162).
Yet this peculiar newspaper notice, under the
headline "Shaking Hands with the Spirit of the
Great Father," referred to the Sioux delegation
that visited Washington *two years later*, in 1872.[21]

On June 1 the Red Cloud delegation arrived in
Washington and was also lodged at the Washington House. The next day the two Sioux delegations
met in the lobby. Despite the tensions between
Spotted Tail and Red Cloud growing out of the
death of Red Cloud's kinsman, Big Mouth, the two
leaders greeted one another amicably, shook
hands, and agreed to do what was best for their
people (p. 154).[22] On June 2 President Grant sent
word to Commissioner Parker that he wished to
see only the Spotted Tail delegation at noon that

21. Poole's diary has not been located, but entries from it are
quoted in John Hudson Poole, *American Cavalcade.* The newspaper story appeared in the *Washington Evening Star,* September 24, 1872, p. 1.

22. "The Indians in Washington," *New York Herald,* June 3,
1870, p. 7.

day, an apparent recognition of the Brule chief's
friendship and loyalty to the United States.

For Spotted Tail and his delegation, this meeting
with the Great Father was the entire purpose of
the trip. As Poole recorded the event, Spotted Tail
made the request they had come for – asking that
their agency be moved from the Missouri River.
The agent wrote: "The President promised Spotted Tail that he should have an agency anywhere
he wanted it, within the Sioux reservation" (p. 168).
From the Indians' perspective, their primary goal
had been met, and they were ready to return home.
Poole reported that the president presented Spotted Tail with a meerschaum pipe, carved with his
monograph, and the newspaper account described
it as having a bowl representing a horse head.[23]

The government officials were not yet ready to
let Spotted Tail leave, perhaps wishing the Whetstone delegates to stay to exert a beneficial influence on Red Cloud and his chiefs. On June 3 the
two delegations met with Secretary of the Interior
Jacob D. Cox and Commissioner Parker, which
proved to be only a ceremonial welcoming of the
newcomers (p. 170–72). On June 4, Commissioner
Parker escorted the delegations to the Arsenal and
Navy Yard, and visited the iron-clad *Monitor* (p.
175–80). The next day was Sunday, and the Indi-

23. "The Indians in Washington," *New York Herald*, June 3,
1870, p. 7.

ans' activities escaped the official record. On Monday evening, June 6, the Sioux delegates attended a gala reception at the White House, replete with cabinet members, congressmen, and foreign diplomats, all accompanied by their wives (p. 181–87).

Only on June 7 was the Red Cloud delegation at last called to the Indian Office for serious business, a review of the articles of the 1868 treaty. Spotted Tail also attended. Curiously, Poole makes no mention of this meeting, which was–from the perspective of the government officials–the crucial session. Red Cloud made a dramatic speech, declaring his desire for peace, but revealing how little he understood of the treaty to which his name was affixed. Spotted Tail spoke at the conclusion of the meeting in support of Red Cloud's plea for presidential pardon of John Richard, Jr., the half-blood Sioux indicted for the murder of a soldier at Fort Fetterman; Red Cloud had brought Richard to Washington as interpreter.[24]

The time was well past for the Whetstone delegates to leave the capital, and on June 8 they were reported to have had a final meeting with the president to pay their respects.[25] The next day Spotted Tail and his delegation had a last long

24. Minutes of meeting with Red Cloud and Spotted Tail delegations, June 7, 1870 (M234, roll 895, C1416).

25. "The Indian Delegations," *New York Herald*, June 9, 1870, p. 3.

meeting with Secretary Cox and Commissioner Parker; Felix Brunot also attended (p. 188–89). The main topic was the Indians' desire to go on their annual buffalo hunt in the Republican River country. Agent Poole urged the necessity of this to supply the Indians' needs, but the officials were unable to make any promises.[26]

Poole left Washington that day with his charges and arrived in the evening at Philadelphia, where they spent the night. The next day, June 10, they were escorted around the city by William Welsh, former president of the Board of Indian Commissioners. As Poole suggested, Welsh had established himself as an independent watchdog of government Indian policy, beginning his work by studying the situation among the Sioux on the Missouri (p. 190).

On June 11 the party arrived in New York, where they were the guests of Charles Stetson, proprietor of the Astor House – once New York's most fashionable hotel, but by 1870 considered outmoded and in decline. That evening the delegation went to Niblo's theater to see Watts Phillips' military drama, "Not Guilty," praised by the *New York Times* for its "general animation," "pictorial qualities," "effective military maneuvering," "bright scenery," and "liberal allowance of music." In short,

26. Minutes of meeting with Spotted Tail delegation, June 9, 1870 (M234, roll 895, C1416).

it could be appreciated without understanding the dialogue. Poole reported that while the Indians enjoyed the spectacle, "they were as undemonstrative as living creatures could be" (p. 196). Interestingly, the *New York Herald* reporter perceived the situation differently: "The theatrical performance greatly interested them, and to the grotesque antics of the drunken soldier in 'Not Guilty' they showed their teeth to gladsome, childish glee."[27]

The next day Spotted Tail was blunt when the reporter interviewed him about the treaty. The Brule leader said, "We do not want the pale-faces. We want our lands. Leave us alone. The Indian does not read and write. He wants his hunting ground. He must be an Indian."[28]

The delegation spent two days sightseeing and on June 13 they boarded the train for Chicago. The *Herald* reporter noted that the Indians' visit "has developed an unexpected kindness on the part of the mass of the people toward the annoyed and swindled tribes of the far West," and expressed the public desire "to protect them from the more than savage incursions of the Western settlers."[29]

When the delegation reached Fort Randall—the Indians laden with presents and riding good

27. *New York Times*, June 12, 1870, p. 4; "Princes of the Prairies," *New York Herald*, June 12, 1870, p. 4.

28. "The Red Men," *New York Herald*, June 13, 1870, p. 8.

29. "The Red Men," *New York Herald*, June 14, 1870, p. 5.

American horses purchased for them in Sioux City–Spotted Tail learned that his favorite wife had died during his absence. All celebration of return was abandoned. The chief gave away everything he had received on his trip east and went into mourning. Arriving back at Whetstone on June 24, Poole seems to have questioned whether the trip had been worthwhile. The Indians, as he repeatedly emphasized, were incapable of comprehending what they saw on their travels, and as Spotted Tail had warned the agent before going, if he told his people truthfully about all he would see, they would not believe him–brand him a liar–and he would lose his following.

Some time after their return, the delegates convened a council and reported on their successes. Poole reported to Governor Burbank on July 4 that the Indians were well pleased with the results of the trip and were anxiously awaiting the arrival of their annuity goods. They wanted to know when they would be allowed to go on their fall buffalo hunt in the Republican River country, which the delegates believed had been promised to them in Washington. And they wanted to know how soon the government would move the agency to its new location up the White River.

Despite the good feelings expressed by the Whetstone delegates as a result of their visit to Washington, the state of affairs in Sioux country remained very much unsettled. Red Cloud

declared while in Washington that at the time he
signed it, he had been told that the 1868 treaty was
only a pledge of peace, and he expressed surprise
and anger when the articles were read to him. He
denounced the treaty as a fraud and gave no assurances that he would move within the reservation
boundaries.[30]

In August, Colonel Franklin F. Flint, commanding Fort Laramie, telegraphed to the commissioner of Indian affairs the rumor reported by visiting
Brule Indians that instead of rations, the Sioux at
Whetstone were receiving "plenty of whiskey
brought by Steamers." When asked for an explana-
tion, Poole could only remind the commissioner
that the sale of alcohol had been "a constant source
of annoyance to all in any way connected with con-
ducting the affairs of this Agency," and he expressed his aggravation at Flint for reporting as
reliable the "ex parte statements of renegade Indians." William Welsh visited Whetstone, as mentioned by Poole (p. 210–14), to investigate the situation, and Colonel Stanley came to the agency to
conduct a military inspection (p. 215). Neither in-
vestigator could blame Poole for the problems at
Whetstone, and Stanley went so far as to write to
the commissioner of Indian affairs: "I venture the

30. Minutes of meeting with Red Cloud and Spotted Tail delegations, June 7, 1870 (M234, roll 895, C1416); Olson, *Red Cloud
and the Sioux Problem,* 105–7.

prediction that many a day will pass after he leaves the agency before the Indians find an agent who will give them the same satisfaction, and look so well to the interests of the U.S."[31]

In his correspondence with Washington, Poole projected a zealousness to see that the Sioux were treated fairly, and in their own best interests as he perceived them. But in his book he lamented that there seemed to be an inverse relationship between degree of first-hand acquaintance with Indians and the clarity with which plans for civilizing them were proposed (p. 23–24). Thus from the perspective of Washington the necessity of adopting a settled way of life based on agriculture was antithetical to continued buffalo hunting, but without the hunts, the Indians lacked the raw materials from which they made most of their tools, clothing, and shelter. Poole's final urgent request that the Whetstone Indians be allowed to go on a buffalo hunt to obtain the "skins and robes and other necessaries which the buffalo supply to them" went unheeded, and was refused by the Indian Office (p. 218).[32]

The issue of moving Spotted Tail's camp up the

31. Flint to Parker (telegram), August 6, 1870 (M234, roll 896, F467, frame 350); Poole to Burbank, Aug. 19, 1870 (M234, roll 896, D1485, frames 212–14); Stanley to Commissioner of Indian Affairs, August 21, 1870 (M234, roll 896, P496, frame 462).

32. Poole to Burbank, July 4, 1870 (M234, roll 895, D1346, frames 145–47).

White River fared little better, and on September 1, Governor Burbank reported to the Indian Office that Spotted Tail was losing patience. Unless the move were made within a month, Spotted Tail claimed, it would be impossible for him to keep his people together and he predicted that many of them would join the northern, nonagency Sioux. On October 14 Poole telegraphed to Commissioner Parker for permission to haul Spotted Tail's supplies to the forks of the White River. The Brules established their winter camp on the White River near the mouth of Big White Clay Creek, and Poole's clerk, Stephen S. Estes (who was married to a Sioux woman), went with them to issue rations and function as subagent.

Captain Poole was nearing the end of his tenure as agent. By the congressional act of July 15, 1870, army officers were prohibited from accepting civil appointments. On October 12 the order was issued at Department of Dakota headquarters to relieve Poole from duty as agent and to place him instead in command of a detachment of some eighty noncommissioned officers and men of the 22nd Infantry at the post at Whetstone Agency. In accordance with Grant's peace policy, the Episcopal Church nominated Poole's successor, John M. Washburn, who took charge on November 18. To him fell the duty of relocating the agency away from the Missouri, which at last took place during the month of June 1871.

In May 1871 Poole married Maria Woodward Pettes in St. Louis, where he had met her the previous winter. Poole had visited the city during late January and early February while on leave from his agency duties at Whetstone. They returned to Fort Randall in June. The military post at Whetstone had become unnecessary after the removal of the Indian agency and the army abandoned it in April 1872. In the summer of 1873 Poole was a member of Colonel Stanley's expedition accompanying the surveyors for the Northern Pacific Railroad across the Sioux reservation and up the Yellowstone Valley in Montana. During the next two years he served at Detroit and New Orleans, but he was transferred back to Montana following the Custer debacle in 1876 and served under Colonel Nelson A. Miles in the campaigns against the Sioux. On May 7, 1877, he participated in the battle of Muddy Creek—Miles' attack on the village of Lame Deer, a Minneconjou Sioux chief. This was Poole's last experience on the Northern Plains.

In subsequent years, Poole's service in the army took him across the continent. In 1880 he returned to New York to look after business interests, and the next year the account of his experiences among the Sioux was published in New York by D. Van Nostrand. What impelled him to prepare his memoir at this time is not recorded, though his book fit into the burgeoning literature on Indian reform. In 1882 Poole was appointed paymaster at Vancouver; in 1887 he was transferred to San Antonio; and in 1891 he was assigned to Cincinnati, where, the next year, he was retired by law at age sixty-four. In retirement Poole was no less nomadic. After his wife's death in 1896 he traveled widely throughout Europe and the United States. On November 30, 1917, he died at his home in Madison, Wisconsin, at the age of eighty-nine. *Among the Sioux of Dakota* was his only book, although his life was memorialized in a biography written by his son, John Hudson Poole.

The republication of Captain Poole's book places a responsibility on the modern reader to understand the work in the context of its time. The book may serve as a model of nineteenth-century white American attitudes toward the American Indians. Poole's experiences with the Sioux doubtless reinforced his perception of them as children. From a modern perspective of cultural anthropology we can appreciate that Poole lacked any apprehension of cultures in the relativistic sense. That this is so comes as no surprise; in fact, he embraced the most popular scientific theories of his day.

Poole believed in social evolution, accepting as self-evident that the social institutions of American Indians—such as their customary law—were like those "of our own remote ancestors" (p. 93). Civilization was a historical process of enlightenment, the end point in a developmental chain.

Poole's evening at the White House led him to ruminate on the differences between the status of women in "savagery" – the lowest social state – and civilization (p. 184). Differential positions on the scale of civilization reflected the groups' historical experiences, not the potential of individuals. Thus Poole cautioned against judging Indians as a class, though he noted that such indiscrimation seemed to be universal: Indians condemned whites as a class, just as much as the reverse (p. 107–8).

Despite his level-headed perspective, rejecting both extremes of the frontiersmen's clamoring for Indian extermination (p. 147) and the easterners' romanticized and guilt-driven philanthropy (p. 152–53), Poole nonetheless affirmed his faith in the superiority of the Anglo-Saxon race, the inevitability of the conflict with the native inhabitants of America, and the necessity for the Indians to accept the consequences if they were to survive in the United States. He suggested that the Sioux might be strong enough to preserve their "customs and mode of life," but only by removing themselves from civilization and remaining in the unsettled portions of western Canada (p. 226–27). Ironically, Poole's book was published in the very year that saw the virtual extinction of the buffalo herds, without which the hunting-based lifestyle could no longer continue.

Bound as he was to a materialistic understanding of the differences among peoples, Poole could only conceive of two possibilities for the future of American Indians: either they would assimilate into the rest of the American population – the goal of official Indian Office policy – or they would become extinct. Nineteenth-century theories of social evolution, blindly accepted as historical fact rather than speculation, failed to consider the possibility that American Indians might endure into the future not by clinging stubbornly to the customs of the past, but by transforming traditions to adapt them to the conditions of modern life.

Among the Sioux of Dakota is not a memorable book for its insight into American Indian culture. For example, Poole utterly failed to achieve any understanding of Sioux religion, admitting that he could see in it only "selfishness and vindictiveness" (p. 75). Despite the book's shortcomings, it preserves almost inadvertently a valuable record of a variety of Sioux customs and beliefs, and it is the preeminent source for understanding the experiences of the Brules and Oglalas at Whetstone Agency. It is also important as a document of the challenges that faced frontier Indian agents as they attempted to put into action government policies to transform the hunting tribes of the Plains into communities of farmers – in the rhetoric of the day, to raise the Plains Indians from savagery to civilization.

Today we condemn the inherent racism and ethnocentrism that formed the intellectual scaffolding of an era seen in retrospect as bigoted and self-satisfied. But just as individuals create ideas, so ideological currents shape individuals; Poole cannot be blamed for the deficiences of post-Civil War Indian policy, nor can he be exonerated as a hapless victim of the times in which he lived. The best that can be said is that he tried conscientiously to do his duty toward the Indians under his charge, within the limitations imposed on him by government policy, frontier politics, and his own understanding of the problems and potentials of his role as agent. He saw the Indians of Whetstone Agency through what may have been their most trying time—their first experiment with reservation life—and in his book he preserved a documentary record of that experience which helps us to reconstruct a rounded picture of life during that stressful time of enforced social and cultural change. Moreover, Colonel Stanley's prediction came all too painfully true: it was many a year before the Sioux at the new Spotted Tail Agency, later called Rosebud, had an agent who gave them as much satisfaction as Captain Poole.

— RAYMOND J. DEMALLIE

AMONG

THE SIOUX OF DAKOTA

EIGHTEEN MONTHS EXPERIENCE

AS AN INDIAN AGENT.

3.—*Fisherman*—Master, I marvel how the fishes live in the sea.
1.—*Fisherman*—Why, as men do a land :
    The great ones eat the little ones.
                                        —SHAKESPEARE.

BY

CAPTAIN D. C. POOLE,

22d Infantry, U. S. A.

1881

CHAPTER I.

IN May, 1869, while stationed at Mcpherson
Barracks, Atlanta, Ga., having just passed
through one of the convulsions resulting in
consolidation of the army by Congress, I received the following order from the Headquarters of the Army:

HEAD QRS. OF THE ARMY,
ADJUTANT GENERAL'S OFFICE,
WASHINGTON, May 7, 1869.

General Orders
No. 49.

By orders received from the War Department the following named officers, left out of
their regimental organizations by the consolidation of the infantry regiments, are, under and
by authority of an Act of Congress organizing
the Indian Department, approved June 30,
1834, hereby detailed to execute the duties of
Indian Superintendents and Agents, and imme-

diately on receiving notice of this order, will
report by letter to the Commissioner of Indian
Affairs, Hon. E. S. Parker, Washington, D. C.,
for assignment to duty and for instructions.

  *   *   *   *   *

  By command of

     GENERAL SHERMAN.
     E. D. TOWNSEND,
      Adjutant General.

  After having reported, in accordance with
this order, there followed from the Interior
Department a letter of instructions, which can
best be understood by reading the following:

    DEPARTMENT OF THE INTERIOR,
    OFFICE OF INDIAN AFFAIRS,
   WASHINGTON, D. C., June 14, 1869.

  SIR: Under authority conferred by the 4th
section of the Act of Congress, approved June
30, 1834, for the organization of the Department
of Indian Affairs, and making it competent for
the President of the United States to require
any military officer to execute the duties of Indian Agent; and in accordance with General
Orders 49, issued from the Head Quarters of
the Army, at Washington, dated May 7, 1869,
detailing you for such duty and directing you
to report to this office for assignment thereto
and for instructions, you are hereby notified
that you are assigned to the position of Agent

for Indians in the Sioux District, located upon a reservation at Whetstone Creek, Dakota Territory.

Having reported here agreeably to the order referred to, you are now instructed to proceed, without unnecessary delay, to your agency, and enter upon duty. You will report to * * * Governor and ex-officio Superintendent of Indian Affairs for Dakota Territory, through whom your official correspondence must be conducted, and through whom you will receive from this office such instructions as from time to time may be deemed necessary.

You will promptly and fully advise the Department of all matters of interest and importance relating to the condition of your agency, make such suggestions or recommendations in reference thereto as in your judgment may be proper, and carry faithfully into effect the regulations of the Department and the instructions that may be given by the Secretary of the Interior, the Commissioner of Indian Affairs, and your Superintendent. As the great object of the Government is to civilize the Indians by locating them in permanent abodes upon suitable reservations, and assisting them that they may sustain themselves, and engage in the pursuits of civilized life, you are earnestly requested to use your best endeavor to advance this humane and wise policy. Hence, you will use every means practicable to inform yourself as fully as possible respecting the condition of the Indians in your charge, and inform the Indian mind, upon every favorable opportunity, with this view and desire of the Government, and thus prepare them to submit to the inevitable change of their mode of life to that more congenial to a civilized state. You will endeavor to keep before their mind the benevolent institutions of the Government, and in your intercourse with them seek to obtain their confidence, and by honest and just dealings secure that peace which it is the wish of all good citizens to establish and maintain. Your success in the accomplishment of the object desired will depend greatly upon the efficiency and discretion to be exercised by you, and in the economical expenditures of the means that may be placed at your disposal; and it is confidently hoped that the result will prove the wisdom and expediency of your appointment for duty so responsible.

* * * * *

Very respectfully,
Your obedient servant,
E. S. PARKER,
Commissioner.

Having digested the order and instructions, and having packed my personal effects and made ready for a start, I turned to the maps to

learn something of my new field of operations.
A large space, marked Dakota, was a blank,
except the rather erratic black line which marks
the progress of the muddy Missouri, as, starting from the southwest in Montana Territory,
it follows nearly all the points of the compass
until it gradually tends towards the southeast
on its way to the Gulf; and a few old Indian
trading posts, dignified by the name of military
stations, Fort So-and-So, but posts which had
never sheltered a soldier returning from dangerous scout or the weary tramp of explora-
tion, and the three genuine United States' posts
—Fort Sully, Fort Randall and Fort Rice.
Fort Buford might have claimed a place, but
then, as now, was generally ignored by map-
makers for Fort Union, an abandoned Indian
trading post, which had its liveliest existence
half a century ago. But any point established
within the last decade was a blank. Turning
to personal inquiry, I elicited about the same
amount of information. The few who had any
knowledge of the land of the Dakotas would
say: "It's a terribly cold country in winter and
melting hot in summer ; no rain ; you can't
raise anything, and, if you do, the grasshoppers will eat it up." Also, however, that when
there was a good season the garrison at Fort
Randall raised a fine crop of vegetables, and
the troops added largely to their company

funds by sales to steamboats, and to the pros-
pectors and miners who floated down the river
from Montana in mackinacs and dugouts.

I also remembered reading rather glowing
accounts of how the Nomads had been moved
from the Platte River and nearness to the Union
Pacific Railroad by that gallant soldier and
eminent Indian manager, General Harney, and
located upon the rich alluvial soil of the bot
tom lands of the Missouri in Dakota; of what
progress they had made in the pursuits of agriculture, the thousands of acres ploughed, the
quantity of grain which would be raised the
coming season, and something near a suggestion that at no distant time they would be
sending a surplus of products to market. But,
then, more was to be learned on this subject
from the Governor and ex-officio Superintendent, whom I was to meet farther on.

Military orders are to be obeyed, and fourteen hundred miles of railroad brought me to
Sioux City, the "jumping off place" of that
day.

From here the stage must be used, or the
steamboat of the Missouri, made to run on
water or moist mud, as the case might be. The
stage was daily, the steamboat not anything as
to time, but casting loose her lines for a trip
up the river whenever a sufficient load was on
board to make it pay, and taking such passen-

gers as might apply and were content to take
the chances of departure. The Sioux City of '69
could not boast of palatial hotels, but was supplied with a few places which might come under
the head of "accommodation for man and
beast," the St. Elmo and Northwestern leading
in dividing the patronage of the traveling public. Stopping at either at this time was sug-
gestive of the thought that it would have been
far better to have gone to the other.

General Harney, with his assistants, was
quartered at the Northwestern. Thinking I
might gain some valuable hints from him as to
my new duties, I sought an interview, and
found him fond of praising the Indians' traits of
character, nevertheless heartily glad to escape
from their immediate presence and companion-
ship, at the same time giving a hint of his
friendly interest in these people by saying,
"They are children, sir, and you must deal
with them as such." When asked if he intended to visit the Indians on the Missouri
again, he was most eloquent and decided in his
peculiar way in replying that he did not; as he
had already made too many promises he could
not fulfill, and did not propose to continue in that
line any longer. The Indians might expect to
see him with a quantity of horses, cows and
chickens for them, but they would not, and
did not.

John H. Charles, genial, good natured and
accommodating, kept the principal store that
supplied the wants of dwellers on the banks of
the upper Missouri. He had everything that
officer, soldier, steamboatman and ranchman
needed, or, if not in store, knew precisely where
to get it, how to send it, and when and how it
could be paid for. He gathered in all the gossip
from up-river forts and agencies, and delighted
in telling the newly arrived the latest *bon mots*,
and recounting the changes that had taken
place.

Coming from the East, Sioux City presented
at this time but few attractions other than the
evidence of its growing importance as the outlet of the upper Missouri country, and the ter-
minal point of a railroad connecting with Eastern civilization.

CHAPTER II.

TORTUOUS COURSE OF MISSOURI—DISTANCE BY RIVER AND
BY STAGE—DISCOMFORTS OF TRAVEL—ARRIVAL IN YANK-
TON.

THE tortuous course of the Missouri is
illustrated by the difference in distance
between Sioux City and Yankton by river and
by stage road. By the former it is two hundred and fifty miles, and by the latter sixty-
five.

The distance by river is only estimated, for
so changing is the channel of this erratic stream
that a steamboat never finds it the same in two
consecutive trips, and even during a single trip
she crosses and re-crosses the river so many
times, that her course can only be compared to
that of the man who went home late from his
club, and complained that it was not the length
of the way, but the width of it, that troubled
him.

The channel, with all its irregularities, preserves one general law, and that is to go from
bank to bank at as acute an angle as possible,

so a steamboat is constantly zig-zaging between the two shores, with such variations of angles as the ever-changing sand bars make necessary. These sand bars are innumerable in low water (which usually prevails), and cause the new-comer to exclaim, "How much dry land there is in this water !"

Deciding, then, upon the stage as the most reliable mode of reaching Yankton, the capital city of Dakota, I am, by previous arrangement with mine host, awakened at the witching hour of three A. M., and with many yawnings and stretchings, prepare for the day's work.

The "mud wagon," complimented by the name of stage, makes its appearance in due time, and it having called around for stray passengers before arriving at the St. Elmo, I find I must consider myself fortunate to obtain a seat inside or out. It actually accommodates four inside and one outside with the driver, but any-where from six to a dozen passengers usually present themselves to be wedged into seats, and occupy the limited space as best they may.

The stage agent leaves us to jam and crowd each other to our hearts' content, while the driver impassively nods in his seat, until the magic words, "All right!" pronounced by the former, set us in motion. We wriggle and twist, draw in one foot and shove out another, but finally, with elbows pinioned and sullen

looks, settle down to the morning ride in
silence ; for fifteen good English miles are to be
gone over before breakfast, and who wants to
talk before coffee? Thus solidly packed, we
sway from side to side, or jounce into a slough
and out in unison with our vehicle, the head
and neck moving upon the shoulders being the
only indication of life.

A stop. The driver exclaims, "Mail!" and
at the same moment a leathern bag strikes the
ground with a thud, near the door by our side.
An easy-going individual, emerging from a
typical Western ranch, takes it and disappears.
The driver is down from his seat, his horses are
watered, we inside twist our necks a little more
than usual, until some one explains, "Mail
station ; half way to breakfast," and then
solemn silence again. The mail bag is returned,
the driver once more in his seat, and we are off.
After napping and nodding a weary time we
make another stop, and here we have a change
of horses, and, at last, breakfast. The more
recent arrivals from the East look around for
washing facilities, and find a tin basin sitting
on a bench outside the house, water to be
dipped from a barrel close at hand, and a general towel which is continually revolved in the
search for a dry spot, or one which has not
done too much previous duty. The towel has
a horsey smell, showing that the stablemen do

not have all the modern improvements in their
retiring rooms.

Breakfast is announced, and, without the least
sign of ceremony, each particular passenger
hurries to the tables as fast as his legs can
carry him, and seating himself, eagerly scans
the different dishes. Some of all within reach
is soon transferred to his plate and dispatched
with no show of dalliance. Muddy coffee, fried
pork and potatoes, and bread and butter form
the repast, eagerly relished and cheerfully paid
for at such price as would secure in the East a
sumptuous meal.

Fresh horses are attached, the passengers re-
packed, each slyly striving to secure more
room to the detriment of his neighbor, and we
are once more on the road.

The stage road leads over the flat, monoto-
nous bottom land of the Missouri, which
usually extends back some four or five miles,
but is occasionally narrowed down by the encroaching bluffs, which, at Elk Point, Vermillion and Yankton, reach to the water's edge.

The passengers occasionally awake to some
little conversation, always commonplace, but
our chief interest centers in the frequent
sloughs, the safe crossing of which is always
more or less a matter of speculation. As we
approach one the driver tightens his reins,
flourishes his whip, and then in we go. The

wheels sink lower and lower to the hubs ; our
motion is gradually retarded, and there is a
general rising of interest among the passengers ;
we nearly stop, then floundering, and splash-
ing, slowly move on, the rims of the wheels
carrying great clods of mud and grass. Finally
we reach more solid ground, and the gentle trot
of our horses speeds us on our way. We pass
Elk Point, Vermillion and Thompson's, "the
Boss Ranch;" we have changes of mail and
changes of horses; and finally, as the sun sends
its last slanting rays over the broad prairie,
distant bluffs and strips of woodland, it is announced that we are approaching Yankton.

A sharp turn or two in the road, indicative
of future streets; a faster trot of our horses; a
sudden stop by a plank platform in front of a
house, and we are at the Merchants' Hotel of
'69. A number of persons emerge from the
hotel, nearly filling the walk, and scan with interest each passenger as we awkwardly leave
the stage and set foot in the Capital of Dakota.

Though farther from the base of supplies,
this hotel was an improvement on any in Sioux
City ; a fair table and comfortable rooms were
welcomed after a hard day's ride.

CHAPTER III.

YANKTON, with perhaps eight hundred
or a thousand souls, had within it the
spirit and enterprise which have built towns
and cities here and there, across our continent,
and it needed no prophetic vision to forecast
the time when it would be a point of importance as the outlet of trade from the upper country. It would be the natural terminus of a railroad, and the headquarters of steamboats used
in the mountain trade of Montana, taking the
place that Leavenworth, Council Bluffs and
Sioux City had each held in its turn.

Here I was to pay an official visit to the Governor and *ex-officio* Superintendent of Indian
Affairs, and accordingly I lost no time in seeking the small dwelling on the river bank, which
I was informed was his headquarters. The
genius of our institutions was illustrated in the
unostentatious surroundings of a territorial

Governor, representing, as he did, the power and dignity of the general Government, but far from the artificial requirements of metropolitan taste. The office which I now entered was a plain, uncarpeted room, furnished with a table, a desk, a revolving chair (gubernatorial), one or two common chairs and a huge spittoon cen· trally situated. On introducing myself I was cordially greeted by the Governor, whom I found to be a genial and kindly disposed official.

Naturally, we at once reverted to the Indians on the reservation at Whetstone Creek, and I expected to hear some wise suggestions with regard to their management, and interesting accounts of them generally. Much to my surprise, the Governor and *ex-officio* Superintendent of Indian affairs acknowledged but a slight acquaintance with them, and knew nothing personally, as he had never been at the Agency. He had had experience with the Omahas in Nebraska, but the wild Sioux of his Territory were a very different people.

I noticed at this time one fact which was afterward confirmed, that those who had been some time associated with Indians assumed to know little of their character, and usually had no plans for their management, or fixed views as to how our Government should treat them. At some time these persons might have had plans and policies, but actual contact had shaken their faith in making Indians first-class citizens and Christians during the time of one administration or even of one life. But a newly-appointed attaché of the Indian Bureau, born and raised in the New England States, perhaps, will unhesitatingly mark out a course to pursue, which will transform a savage into an enlightened citizen, surely within the period of his administration. Thus " distance lends enchantment to the view."

In the midst of our interesting conversation a steamboat whistle was heard. In an instant the Governor seized his hat and was hastening toward the door. I asked what was the matter, expecting to hear that his office was in flames, or some like accident.

"Didn't you hear that whistle?" he exclaimed. "There's a steamboat coming ; come on." I joined him, and we hurried toward the river, where a steamboat could be seen in the distance, making slow headway against the current, though under full head of steam, as shown by the black smoke rolling out of her chimneys, and the white puffs of steam issuing from her escape pipes.

The whole town seemed to be approaching the landing, and I was informed that they always turned out when a boat arrived from below ; some having actual business, some moved by curiosity, and all impelled by the desire for some excitement which this event seemed to supply.

The "Evening Star," as the steamer proved to be, was en-route for Fort Sully, and having had sufficient experience with the stage, I concluded to try the river. The "Evening Star," to be sure, had been a week on the way from Sioux City, and no one knew how long it would take her to reach Whetstone Creek reservation; but the saving of time ceases to be an object as you recede from civilization. The tri-weekly stage made the distance from Yankton to Fort Randall, about seventy-five miles, within fifteen hours, but the steamboat promised more comfort, if less speed.

I found the Missouri River steamboat was not commodious, nor luxuriously furnished in any way for the accommodation of passengers. The small staterooms had scarcely enough in them for comfort; while the table was supplied with the coarsest food; fried liver and onions, fried bacon, thick coffee and hot, sodden biscuits formed the principal articles of diet. Milk and butter were luxuries by no means common.

As we progressed up the river, the captain, pilot, mate and all hands seemed to direct their entire attention towards making the "Evening Star" push her way over sand bars, and to finding that part of the river which contained

the greatest depth of water. This was often a
hidden mystery, requiring for its solution hours
of diligent search in a small boat manned with
a crew and pilot, who, with sounding pole in
hand, fathomed all parts of the river, while the
steamboat "lay to" with her nose gently
pushed against the bank, and her wheels kept
in just sufficient motion to hold her against the
strong current. The pilot, having fully recon-
noitered, would return to his elevated house
and jingle a bell. A louder noise of puffing
steam would be heard, and an attempt at further progress made. Often this selected channel would prove a failure ; the boat would
gradually "slow up" as she came in contact
with the sandy bottom, and then come to a dead
stop. But the master of the craft was equal to
the occasion, and would issue the startling
order, "Plant a dead man !"

At this a boat would be manned and a log
carried on shore some distance above the point
where the steamboat was stuck. Here a line
from the steamboat was made fast to the log,
which was firmly buried in a deep hole dug for
the purpose. The end of the line on board was
made fast to the capstan, a full head of steam
applied to the latter, and drawing heavily upon
the line, which was wound up on the rapidly
revolving capstan, we would be gradually
dragged over the sand bar.

This failing, recourse was had to the huge wooden spars, shod with iron points, which were suspended by lines and pulleys on either side of the forward deck. When needed, their lower ends were thrown overboard, the lines from their upper ends fastened by a system of blocks and pulleys to the donkey engine, and the latter put in motion by an order to "Go ahead on the nigger."   In this way the steamboat was on legs for the time being.

With these auxilaries, the "deadman" and capstan, the spars and donkey engine, the craft was generally "grasshoppered" over the sand bars, but when these failed downright disappointment brooded over the navigator's face, and "double tripping" was the last resort. This was the simple process of leaving half the freight on shore; after which the lightened steamboat could pass over the shallow water to a point above. Here the remainder of the freight must be unloaded, while she went back for the first half; and then on her return, of course, all must be once more taken on board. A slow and laborious process, which it was no wonder was the dread of the river men.

The passengers all seemed to take the liveliest interest in the boat's progress, and many were the comments on the probability of arriving at some woodyard at a certain time; or the

passing of some bad place in the river, with
which they had had previous experience.

And so amid many doubts and uncertainties
we held to our course, passing Bon Homme,
Santee Sioux agency, Ponca agency, and Yankton Sioux agency, and finally arriving at Fort
Randall, where we landed some freight and
were visited by its occupants, officers and men
of the 22nd Infantry.

Here I met Captain A. E. Woodson, who had
preceded me at the Agency, and who was acting Commissary for issuing supplies there. He
gave me my first insight into the condition of
affairs among the Indians ; the want of suitable
shelter for supplies on hand and to arrive ; the
number of the Indians and their various wants ;
and their anxiety to see their new agent, who
they supposed was coming with all manner of
good things to make their "hearts glad." He
also exhibited a couple of leaden bullets, picked
up in his sleeping room. They had been fired
through the door from a rifle in the hands of
some impatient savage, who thus showed his
disgust at the management of affairs in general,
and the manager in particular.

Not an over-bright picture of a quiet and
peaceful life, while teaching the aborigines the
beneficence of the Government.

CHAPTER IV.

ARRIVAL AT WHETSTONE CREEK RESERVATION—ITS LOCATION
AND DESCRIPTION—EXTENT OF THE SIOUX RESERVATION
UNDER TREATY OF 1868—DIFFERENT BANDS—NUMBER
OF SIOUX SUPPLIED AT WHETSTONE.

STILL following the fortunes of the "Evening Star," I once more embarked, and next day, toward evening, the low, uncouth buildings of Whetstone Creek reservation appeared. Whites and Indians could be seen making their way leisurely toward the landing, moved by the curiosity which seems to pervade all dwellers on the Missouri River, to see a steamboat of any size or description, and more especially one coming from below.

This spot was utterly devoid of the wild picturesqueness supposed to be incident to its location and inhabitants. The "first bench," or level ground extending immediately back from the river, was some eighty rods wide, and covered in most places with a thick growth of willows interlaced with wild vines. A sharp rise of six or eight feet led to the

"second bench," another level stretch of
ground which extended back to the bluffs,
covered near the river with an undergrowth
of oak, but soon running into prairie. This
rich bottom land followed the course of the
river for some four miles, but was cut off
above and below by the bluffs, which at these
points circled into the very bank. Whetstone
Creek, fringed with a very small growth of
timber, broke through the range of bluffs from
the west and joined the Missouri, while farther
south Scalp Creek did the same. These creeks
contained running water only after severe rains,
soon subsiding, and having nothing in their
dry beds save "water holes" at long distances.
An island in the river, a short distance from the
agency, furnished cottonwood logs for fuel and
for building. The pocket of land thus enclosed
by the river and the bluffs, contained about two
thousand acres of rich alluvial soil, and, in
addition to this, Whetstone Creek bottom
lands, suitable for cultivation, extended some
distance farther back.

Near the edge of the second bench a row of
rough log buildings was ranged, the carpen-
ter's shop, blacksmith's shop, two medium-
sized storehouses, an office and council room in
one, a dispensary, the barn and stables, and, to
the left and towards the river, the saw mill;
these comprising all the agency buildings.

Immediately back some irregularly located log huts occupied the ground, exciting a faint suspicion that there was some intention of a street. The rest of the ground back to the bluffs was occupied by Indian Tepees. The trader's store, holding a central position, was by far the most pretentious building of all.

This spot of ground with its buildings was known in Dakota as the Whetstone Agency, and was regarded by most persons as the reservation of the Indians located there. Even in the Interior Department it seemed to be understood that the Indians here were confined within narrow and well-defined bounds. My instructions stated that I was to be agent for Indians in the Sioux District, *located upon a reservation*, etc. With the Poncas or the Santee Sioux, whose reservations contained only a few thousand acres each, agency and reservation were almost synonymous terms. With the Indians at Whetstone it was entirely different. My first information after coming in contact with them, was that in place of being pent up within narrow bounds, they claimed, and rightfully, all the land from the northern boundary of Nebraska to the forty-sixth parallel of latitude, and from the right bank of the Missouri to the one hundredth and fourth degree of longitude west ; a vast area of land, containing at a low estimate forty-six thousand square miles, or nearly thirty millions of acres, over which they were free to roam at will.

Under the treaty of 1868 they held this reservation in common with those other bands of the Sioux nation who had had their homes west of the Missouri. The estimated number of the nations was at this time twenty-eight thousand, which would be about one person to every thousand acres, or each man, woman and child could occupy an area of nearly two square miles. A division by families would give much more elbow room. A large estimate would make only five thousand six hundred homes required, and thus give an allowance of over five thousand acres to each family. Of what use would such vast area be in teaching Nomads the first principles of civilization, and helping them to form permanent homes? As a hunting park it was equally a failure. The buffalo ranged south, west and north of this tract of country ; and the Indians could not subsist upon the small game, such as antelope, deer and mountain sheep, which were found in moderation. This was apparently understood by the framers of the treaty, as it was expressly provided therein, that whenever the buffalo could be found on any lands north of the North Platte and on the Republican Fork of the Smokey Hill River, the Indians should be allowed to hunt them.

The possession of this princely domain was the cause of much misunderstanding and discontent. It was given to these uncivilized Indians in solemn treaty, stipulating that no person except officers and agents of the Government should ever be permitted to pass over, settle upon or reside in the territory described. But already in one short year was proved the utter impossibility of keeping in good faith, and protecting from encroachment, the terms of this immense contract. Another difficulty was the inability to make the Indians understand anything of imaginary geographical lines. They knew nothing of such nice distinctions, but had a general idea that their possessions extended west as the crow flies, to the Wind River mountains of Wyoming, and northwest through the eastern part of Montana to the British possessions.

The Brulé and Ogallala Sioux at the agency numbered at this time about fifteen hundred souls. Most of them, having separated themselves from their former chiefs, were known as the "loafer band," and were living in huts and adjacent tepees under the chieftainship of Big-mouth, the most loquacious and persistent beggar that ever walked. A short distance above the agency was a small collection of tepees ruled by Swift Bear; below were Standing Elk, a Brulé, and his band, while a mile or so back from the agency, on Whetstone Creek, Fire Thunder, an Ogallala, swayed by his eloquence and valor the inhabitants of fifteen or twenty tepees. A few Cheyennes were intermarried with these different bands, and affiliated with them. Mingled with all the bands were a number of white men who had married with the Indians, and were recognized by them as entitled to share in any grants or donations of the Government. These white men had been associated with the Sioux for a number of years, coming among them at first as hunters and trappers for fur companies, afterward as guides to military and other expeditions, and then as traders and interpreters.

Spotted Tail, a Brulé Sioux, who had always held himself aloof from the "loafers" at the agency, kept his camp of from three hundred and fifty to four hundred lodges at a point as remote as the necessity of procuring supplies would permit, usually from thirty to fifty miles distant. I soon became acquainted with the principal members of these different communities.

CHAPTER V.

INSPECTION OF PROPERTY FOR USE OF INDIANS—AGRICUL-
TURAL IMPLEMENTS—RATIONS—CULTIVATED LAND, ITS
PRODUCTS—WANT OF INTEREST BY INDIANS—FIRST AT-
TEMPT TO CULTIVATE THE SOIL.

AMONG my first duties after arriving at the
agency was the inspection of the property, in store and in use, belonging to the Government and for the benefit of the Indians.
This survey revealed very many useful articles,
such as would be required in the erection of
buildings, and the permanent establishment of
a community, such as a growing Western village. There were material for furnishing blacksmith's shop and saw mill, and connections for
grinding corn ; ordinary wagons and carts, and
huge log carts with immense wheels. These
latter articles were a little superfluous, as the
wheels were so far apart that they would not
track in any known roadway, and a log corresponding to the size of the truck could not be
found in the Territory. Besides these were
great wagons known as "prairie schooners,"

with a carrying capacity of eighty hundred weight or more. A large assortment of agricultural implements clearly indicated the desire on the part of the purchaser for the speedy arrival of the red man at a most advanced stage of scientific farming. There were patent corn planters and grain drills, reapers and horse rakes for harvesting the grain, threshing machines and fanning mills, cultivators and harrows, breaking ploughs and cross ploughs, scythes, pitchforks and rakes. In fact, some of everything contained in a first-class agricultural implement establishment. A good assortment of drugs and medicines arrayed on shelves in the dispensary showed that the healing art had not been neglected. Two storehouses were filled with substantial provisions, consisting of flour, corn, bacon, sugar, coffee, salt and soap. There were also yokes of oxen and horses and mules. The expenditures had been lavish, if not always judicious. A number of acres had been broken in various parts of the agency ground, and the different plats surrounded by fences, all the work of the Government employés, as an encouraging start for the Indians. Some of these plats of ground were worked by the white men before mentioned, whose squaw wives attracted an endless number of relatives around their homes, only limited by the amount of provisions on hand. The lord of the forest

and prairie was often seen watching the process of ploughing and cultivating performed by
his white relation, as he leaned against the
fence or lay on the ground in the shade, as unconcerned a looker-on as could be found;
seemingly with no thought of ever being obliged
to engage in such pursuit himself.

The formidable array of agricultural implements seemed also to fail to awaken any enthu-
siasm in the red man's breast; never in all my
subsequent experience did I see one observing
the construction of the more intricately con-
trived machines, nor standing behind a plough
(as who has not seen a farmer at a country fair)
holding its handles while turning it from side
to side, with a countenance expressive of the
longing to see the mellow soil roll away from
its polished share.

An inspection of the agency farm, to be sure,
showed a sickly array of the products of hus-
bandry. The wheat, after due preparation of
the ground, had been sown early, and had
sprung up bountifully under the warm sun and
spring rains, but by the middle of June the
rains ceased, the ground became parched and
dry, and the wheat having attained a height of
four or five inches, headed out and completed
its growth in this dwarfed state; the straw
being so short that it could not be harvested
with the most approved machine. The corn

field was more promising. Here the Indian's
interest was aroused, for green corn is one of
his failings, and this crop must succeed. So
he threw all his energy into this branch of
farming, and sent his squaw forth to labor in
planting and hoeing and caring for the same.
The corn furnished for planting was the variety
known as Ree, or squaw corn. It has adapted
itself to the short and fitful season of the
Northwest, coming to perfection for roasting
ears in six weeks, and thus escaping the midsummer droughts and early frosts. But, alas!
a portion of a large army of grasshoppers de-
scended from the skies, and in less than half a
day devoured the corn, leaving the stalks as
bare as fishing rods. Potatoes had also been
planted, but the potato bug was on hand,
apparently having been waiting from time
immemorial for the appearance of his well-
loved vine.

Nature seems to resent the first attempts to
cultivate the soil in this far-off land, and
turns upon the hardy intruder her whole battery of weapons. Terrible rain storms delug-
ing the land, and often mixed with hail of
sufficient size to destroy vegetation and en-
danger animal life; the waterspout and wild
tornado; the scourge of the locust, the grass-
hopper and the beetle.

But if he be patient, and continue to turn

aside the water-shed of nature formed by the close-matted roots and grass of the broad prairie, uncovering the rich black mold, he will be rewarded by a gradual change in climate; for the rain absorbed by the cultivated soil will be given back into the air, again returning in dews and gentle showers. But this is a lesson not easily taught the Indian, who has a childlike interest in the present and small care for the future.

CHAPTER VI.

ACCORDING to custom, a council of the
principal chiefs and warriors must be
called, to announce my arrival in a formal
way. Word was sent to the various representatives through the interpreter; and the old medicine man of the village was also employed to
visit the different camps, and, as he journeyed,
to announce in his stentorian voice the desire of
the agent for a council. There was no danger
of a failure as to audience. Besides the incent-
ive offered by the opportunity for forensic dis
play, always attractive to these people, there
was the accompanying feast.

Preparations were made by erecting a council
lodge, and issuing extra rations of beef and
coffee. The latter were prepared by the squaws
and carried to the lodge, where they were taken
in charge by some of the young aspirants for
future honors.

A general stir among the denizens of the

agency marked an unusual degree of interest in the coming event. Extra paint was applied, and the gayest attire donned, together with the usual complement of weapons, consisting of bows and quivers and the latest improved fire-arms. Spotted Tail having arrived from the prairie with some of his principal braves, all assembled at the appointed place. The chiefs on such occasions were exceedingly punctilious as to their seats in council, the principal one always taking the highest place, and the others following in order of their importance, which was tacitly recognized according to the number of their followers.

Having entered the lodge, they seated themselves on the ground upon their blankets and buffalo robes, and patiently waited to be served with plates and tin cups. The meat and coffee, which make the feast, were then passed around by humble followers of the chiefs. After due time the plates and kettles were removed, and the pipe, filled and lighted, passed from one to another for a smoke, each taking a few whiffs before parting with it. The feasting and smoking were done in a very deliberate manner, the chiefs often speaking with each other in low tones, as if exchanging some views on the coming discussion. This running conference gradually dropped into a dead silence, when it was understood the talk was to commence. Being called upon, I related to them the old story ; that their Great Father in Washington desired to do all in his power for them ; that he wished them to remain at some fixed point, learn to cultivate the soil, and have permanent homes, where they could be taught the ways of the white man, have churches and school houses, and eventually become prosperous and happy. This part of my talk elicited many "hows" from the audience, as visions of ease and abundance always did, but I met with less approval when I went on to make them acquainted with orders lately received from Washington, to the effect that they must remain on their reservation, and should they leave it, would do so at the peril of being driven back by soldiers. All this was duly interpreted into the Sioux language, sentence by sentence, by the interpreter. After a suitable time the principal chief, Spotted Tail, rose from his seat and made the first remarks, of course in his native language. Spotted Tail, though never very eloquent, was direct and forcible, and usually to the point. He was glad to see his new agent, and wanted the horses, oxen and cows promised to his people in the treaty ; he wanted some powder and lead for his camp, to use in hunting deer, antelope, etc.; he had had an agent while on the Platte River who had given him everything he had asked for, and he hoped I would prove equal to him ; that his people were poor, and needed blankets, clothes, axes and kettles.

These remarks were received with many " hows " from Spotted Tail's party. The other chiefs then followed in a similar strain, and with such variations as their native oratory could invent. I promised to do all in my power, and the council broke up with seeming good will on both sides.

Many of these untutored savages showed themselves models of manly bearing and deportment. The chiefs were generally above the average height of white men, erect, full-chested, strong limbed, and with small hands and feet. They were natural orators, and always at home as they rose to speak in council ; standing in a finely poised attitude, their blankets drawn over one shoulder, the other left bare, giving full play to their graceful gestures. They dealt largely in metaphor, drawn from their associations with natural objects, and, when speaking of the wants of their simple lives and of past promises still unfulfilled, were truly eloquent, and seldom failed to impress their views of right upon those in council, whether at their own homes, or, as I subsequently learnt, in the presence of the chief authorities at Washington. In this and following councils they invariably acted with great decorum, and conducted their deliberations with due regard for the feelings of others, provided the subject under consideration was one that in any way tended to the advancement of their present interests. Some remote benefit did not interest them. A divided council was often disturbed by its young members, after the manner of their more cultivated white brethren.

The older chiefs, however, had much leniency for the young men. A young brave, having returned from a successful foray, and his exploits having been duly announced in camp by the songs of the women and the devotees of the scalp dance, would feel his new made honors, and appearing in council would be accorded a place and an opportunity to make his maiden speech. Although the aspirant often failed, his hearers treated him with great consideration, and seldom intimated that he was not equal to the occasion.

CHAPTER VII.

MANNER OF ISSUING FOOD TO THE INDIANS—COST OF SAME.

AN all-important part of my duty, and one which had to be entered upon at once, was issuing food from the store houses. The Indians knew that it was stored away for their use, and, following out their improvident habits of eating to repletion when they had abundance, regardless of how more could be obtained when the present supply was exhausted, did not relish being placed on a regular allowance. It was a constant source of annoyance to me, on account of the continual complaints that the amount received fell far short of their actual necessities; and, as there was a well-founded belief that they were receiving sufficient, many and long were the interviews on the subject.

Big Mouth, an Ogallala chief and a relative of the renowned Red Cloud, being the nominal chief of the "loafer" Indians at the agency, was always eloquent upon the subject. He was round and plump as any city alderman, yet his favorite theme was to enlarge upon the fact that he was starving, and gradually fading away from lack of food.

The Supply Department had fixed the daily ration for each person, irrespective of age, as follows:

One and one-half pounds of fresh beef, one-quarter of a pound of corn or meal, one-half of a pound of flour, four pounds of sugar to one hundred persons, two pounds of coffee to one hundred persons, and one pound of salt and one pound of soap when necessary. Four times each month three-quarters of a pound of bacon to each person was issued in lieu of beef.

Big Mouth did not possess the authority necessary to dictate a proper subdivision, so, in order to secure an equal division, and to provide for the old and infirm and the young and helpless at the agency, a census of families was taken, and as complete a record of numbers was kept as possible. Rations were issued every five days. Before the issue, each head of a family was required to procure a ticket at the agency office, upon which was stated the number of persons in his family and the gross amount of each part of the ration due; and on its being received and taken to the store house, the amount called for could be obtained. An ordinary family of, say, seven persons, would receive, each five days, fifty-two and one-half pounds of fresh beef, or, in lieu of beef, twenty-six and one-quarter pounds of bacon; seventeen and one-half pounds of flour; eight and three-quarters pounds of meal or corn; seven pounds of sugar, and three and one-half pounds of coffee, etc. As some members of such a family were usually young children, it will be seen that this allowance gave a very fair play to the gastronomic abilities of the adults. The women invariably attended to procuring the supplies and conveying them to the tepees, the head of the family making his appearance only when he thought the amount received was not equal to the number of persons to be fed in his lodge. This was the order of proceeding with Big Mouth's band.

Swift Bear, having his people separated from the others, and having full authority over them, was allowed to have the gross amount of his rations each five days, and subdivided the same in his camp. Fire Thunder was granted the same privilege for the same reason. These two sub-chiefs were continually drawing away from the authority of Big Mouth such as became dissatisfied with his influence at the agency. Obtaining their supplies separately gave them great advantage over him, as they were on this account able to give grand feasts. Thus I was enabled to suppress the doughty warrior and chief, and curb his arrogance.

Spotted Tail and his sub-chiefs, Two Strike,

Black Bear and others, were no less interested in the supplies for their camp. These rations were not only given to them, but transported by the Government for them to their camp, which was generally at least fifty miles distant. This transportation was always a matter of discussion. There were from one to two thousand ponies constantly in possession of Spotted Tail's people, which could have been used in packing the rations to his camp. But I never succeeded in interesting him in the subject, and was obliged to continue the employment of a train of wagons for the purpose.

Spotted Tail's rations were issued once in ten days, and a day or two before the issue he usually arrived with his retinue to suggest changes in the amounts of the different parts of the ration. Neither he nor his people could understand why an exact amount of each article should be issued to each person, regardless of preferences. Some did not want meal or corn, but in their place more beef; some wanted more bacon and less beef, or more coffee and sugar as equivalent for less flour.

But with the Supply Department a ration meant the fixed quantity of each article, and any deviation from it would have been a never-ending source of trouble in the settlement of my accounts, no matter how much I might have saved by decreasing and increasing accord-

ing to circumstances, keeping at the same time
within the aggregate. Spotted Tail always
clamored for more beef cattle and bacon, and
always had plausible reasons why more should
be sent him, ably seconded in this by his at-
tendants. He showed true trafficking qualities,
asking for an increase of ten or fifteen head of
cattle and three or four sides of bacon, and
gradually coming down to be quite satisfied
with one or two cattle and half a side of bacon.
But, in spite of my utmost efforts, the issues
had a gradually increasing tendency.

The " talks," having to be interpreted from
side to side, consumed a great deal of time.
They took place in the agency office, and were
also attended by the agency chiefs, Big Mouth,
Swift Bear, Fire Thunder and Standing Elk,
who smoked and conversed with their friends
from the prairie. Generally, after Spotted Tail
and his party had departed, they would take a
hand themselves at trying to get an increase of
rations for their people, thus showing the latter
how zealous they were in looking after the
interests of their adherents.

These discussions in reference to rations
were usually good-natured, but occasionally
Big Mouth would insinuate that all the rations
in the store house belonged to the Indians, or,
if there were no other chief of importance present, he would boldly announce that they all

belonged to him, and that if I were not more
liberal he would go and help himself. But he
always changed his mind before carrying this
threat into effect, for Fire Thunder and
Swift Bear would be informed of his design,
and would immediately set a guard of their
own over the store houses and take occasion to
squelch Big Mouth for his temerity.

If Spotted Tail had this feeling about his
allowance, he never showed it, and, when met
with the argument that large additions to the
amount due to his people would perhaps de-
prive others of their supply, would express
himself satisfied with such small increase as I
could justly make.

Hospitality was certainly one of the cardinal
virtues of these people, and often led to a
scarcity of supply at some lodge, where it had
been too bountifully practiced. But, then, the
inmates knew that others had abundance, and
they would make the rounds, going from camp
to camp, and thus make matters equal.

There were many arrivals at Spotted Tail's
camp and at the agency from Red Cloud's
camp, and from other agencies, besides constant going to and fro of Indians from the hostile camps at this time in existence, all of which
tended to disturb the food supply, and rendered it almost impossible to keep an accurate
census. There were estimated to be in Spotted

Tail's camp two thousand and fifty Indians, and at the agency one thousand five hundred and fifty, including half breeds and whites, making a total of three thousand seven hundred men, women and children. This number was soon increased to four thousand.

These rations were issued to these Indians at a cost to the Government of about thirty thousand dollars a month. But this grand beneficence was never appreciated by them. They seemed to take it as a matter of course. There was no question in their minds as to the continuance of the supply; the only thing that troubled them was the restriction to a daily allowance. They would have preferred to make one grand feast, and trust to luck for more. They had given up the buffalo, and their Great Father was bound to feed them, because they seemed to think he had gotten the best of the bargain; and, as this was part of the policy now in operation — that it was cheaper to feed them than to fight them—perhaps the Indians were right in their conclusions.

CHAPTER VIII.

INDIANS LOOKING FOR ANNUITY GOODS—LARGE NUMBER OF
INDIANS AND SMALL QUANTITY OF GOODS—A DISSATIS-
FIED NOMAD.

I WAS soon made aware that the Indians
had been promised an abundance of blankets and Indian goods, which they had been
looking for since the opening of navigation, and
now it was midsummer and still they had not
come. Upon investigation it was found that,
although Indians were known to be in existence at this point, none had been purchased for
them, much less shipped. The Indians at
Yankton agency, some forty miles down the
river, were receiving their annual supply, or
"annuities;" so also were their friends up the
river at the Crow Creek agency, a hundred
miles away, and of course these facts were well
known to the Indians at Whetstone.

After a strenuous effort on my part, and the
representation of the fact that the Indians
would almost certainly abandon the agency if
they were thus slighted, the matter was taken

in hand by the Governor and *ex-officio* Superintendent of Indian Affairs. He came up the river on the steamboat on which the annuities for Crow Creek were loaded, and, meeting a downward bound boat some distance above Whetstone, transferred a portion of the goods to it, and they were finally landed at the latter point. This conciliated the Indians, who had begun to feel that their hearts were growing bad on account of the neglect of their Great Father in Washington, who was the only authority superior to the agent whom they ever mentioned ; Superintendent, Commissioners and Secretary being totally ignored by them. The arrival of the annuities was soon known among the different camps, and there was at once a perceptible increase in numbers, the same kind of liberality being customary on these occasions as is shown when an unusual supply of food is on hand. They presented their guests with some portion of their gifts, always expecting an equivalent in return should the opportunity present itself, the polite thing being to increase a little the return gift.

The Sioux treaty provided that these people should be not only fed, but clothed for a period of three years ; after which it was supposed by some exceedingly sanguine individuals (remaining at a long distance and necessarily drawing a long bow) that they would become self-supporting from the surplus products of farming. Accordingly, they had a right to expect these annuities.

There were at the agency, and in Spotted Tail's camp, as has been said, three thousand seven hundred Indians, fully two-thirds of whom were men and women grown to such estate as to require blankets. Of these two thousand four hundred, there were probably one thousand two hundred women who would want, in addition, new dresses. The goods, when opened, were found to consist of two hundred and fifty-six blankets, five hundred and forty-eight yards of calico, and a small number of axes, hatchets, kettles and butcher knives. The disparity between the number of Indians to be supplied and the quantity of goods received made an exceedingly interesting problem to be solved, each one of these people having the natural desire to receive some gift. They had been promised to be clothed, and according to their ideas this meant, for the man a blanket, some dark blue cloth for leggins, and a narrow strip of red cloth to bind about the loins, of sufficient length to trail upon the ground ; and for the woman a short, loose frock, close-fitting leggins, and a blanket, if she could get it, it being understood that the man must be properly dressed first.

The quantity of goods being so small, I de-

cided to make the distribution to the lodges
without particular reference to the number in
each. In this manner each family might receive something. Accordingly, the chiefs were
called upon to give the number of tepees in
their respective camps, and, as is invariably the
case on such occasions, all, without exception,
magnified largely their numbers ; but as they
did it in about the same proportion, the result
was not materially affected.

These preliminaries having been completed, a
day was appointed for the distribution, and the
forms of law complied with by advising and
asking the commanding officer of the nearest
military post to be present and witness the distribution. At the appointed time the chiefs
and head men presented themselves with their
followers in large numbers, with the exception
of Spotted Tail, who came with only a few warriors to escort his share to his camp, where he
would himself distribute it. The goods were
taken to a large open space, and placed in lots
corresponding to the number of chiefs, whose
people, principally represented by squaws,
occupied the foreground of the circle, which
was large enough for all to witness the distribution and enjoy the full benefit of publicity.
Each chief, entering the circle with a few of his
warriors, made the distribution to his own people, calling each representative of a family by

name, and giving him such share as he thought proper. At the same time the squaws accompanied the distribution with their discordant songs.

Although the Indians had exhibited a vast amount of interest upon the receipt of their goods, and had advocated their respective claims to large shares of the same; counted the number of packages on arrival and watched over them while in store, and up to their final disposal; yet when the distribution was once made, small as was the share which fell to each family, it proved generally satisfactory, and little complaint was made. The chiefs also expressed themselves satisfied when signing the papers to show they had received the articles sent.

One head of a family, however, felt himself aggrieved by his chief, who had not satisfied his cupidity, and manifested his resentment in rather a disagreeable manner. At daybreak Captain Woodson and myself, who occupied adjoining rooms in a log building, were aroused by the report of a rifle and the peculiar whiz and pat of a ball, which passed through my door, knocked the mud and chinking out of the partition wall between our rooms, and finally rolled on the floor. It was followed by two others, which careered about our apartments until they spent themselves, fortunately not doing much damage. The fusillade was accompanied by a short speech in Sioux, but as neither of us understood the language, that part was lost. Upon inquiry of the interpreter, however, it was found to be anything but complimentary to the agent.

After this little outbreak the Indian folded his tepee, and silently stole away to some of the hostile camps, existing in Montana, in the Rosebud and Powder River valleys.

CHAPTER IX.

PAWNEE SCOUTS DESTROY SIOUX CAMP—MOURNING WOMEN
AND MEN—PAWNEE SCALPS, TRIUMPHAL PROCESSION.

DURING the month of July an unusual excitement was created among the Indians by the arrival of a number of their friends in great distress, the survivors of a small camp that had been attacked and destroyed by some Pawnee scouts in the employ of the Government.

A few Sioux, with their friends the Cheyennes, supposing that they had the right to hunt buffalo on the Republican River in Western Kansas (as they had under their treaty), had gone with their families and lodges from Spotted Tail's camp and the agency to hunt. While so engaged, and after having accumulated quite a quantity of buffalo meat and robes, they had been surprised and attacked by their hereditary enemies, the Pawnees, a number of them killed, and their lodges and the products of the chase destroyed. Those who escaped returned to the agency in great destitution, and related their misfortunes to their friends, whose violent sympathy well illustrated the habits of these people when in grief.

The squaws who were related to those killed, and their female friends, commenced the mourning by singing or chanting their funeral dirges. Their powerful voices were raised in piercing cries, more animal than human, and they gave emphasis to their deep sorrow by a peculiar quavering of the voice when dwelling upon the highest and most prolonged notes, filling the air with discordant sounds, more wild than the howl of prairie wolves.

This noisy demonstration was usually commenced by one voice proceeding from some lodge, and this was a sign that the principal person in it had been sadly bereaved, and that his favorite squaw was ready to begin the usual ceremonies. Sympathizing women at once gathered around the tepee and joined in the funeral chant. While it continued the squaw inside proceeded to give them the contents of the lodge, robes, blankets, pots, kettles, and provisions—in fact everything it contained, all the time singing the praises of the departed. The women as they received these mourning gifts swelled still louder their piercing cries, and remained until everything was disposed of, sometimes the very lodge itself.

To a disinterested spectator of these scenes,

it looked as if those engaged in them were not moved by pure sympathy alone in their demonstrations of grief, but were influenced by a desire to obtain what were to them valuable gifts.

The real mourner was the man. He often cut off his long hair in which he took great pride, allowed his ponies and his best blanket to be given away, and appeared in a buffalo robe or blanket of the poorest quality, old and worn. His bright-beaded leggins were discarded, together with his finely embroidered moccasins. Bare-legged, bare-footed, without paint, his face, arms, and legs often smeared with mud, he fasted, and seldom appeared in public, trying to seclude himself from the world, and could truly be said to wear "sackcloth and ashes."

After the first demonstrations of grief were over, the women had spasmodic periods of mourning, commencing their cries apparently when some incident recalled the memory of the departed. In addition to their noisy demonstrations, they often, as a farther token of grief, gashed their arms and legs, with knives, making the blood flow freely.

The death of an Indian at the hands of an enemy was sure to arouse a spirit of revenge among the whole band to which he belonged, and measures were at once inaugurated to wipe

out their sorrow and bring joy and gladness to
the camp by shedding the blood of their enemies. The young men secluded themselves in
a medicine lodge, presided over by a medicine
man Here they clandestinely met and made
medicine, preparing themselves for the war
path by long dances and by the incantations of
the medicine man, who fortified them for the
dangers of the deadly encounter by continually
demonstrating to them that they could not be
killed. He would follow them through camp
discharging his loaded rifle at them, the ball, of
course, always failing to hit the mark; or, coming upon one of them suddenly, he would shoot
at point blank range of a few feet with the
same happy result. To them the medicine was
good, and they thus became invulnerable.

Being informed that the Indians under my
charge were preparing to avenge the killing of
their friends by the Pawnee scouts, I took
measures to dissuade them from such a course
by calling a council, and reminding the chiefs
of the order about leaving the reservation without permission for hunting or any other purpose. They became satisfied that their friends
had been injudicious in hunting so far away
from the agency, but at the same time could
not be prevailed upon by any inducement
offered to interfere with the young men's
preparations for the war path ; nor could it be

found out who were really to engage in the undertaking. The matter was duly reported to the Department, and for a time the excitement subsided.

It was renewed by the arrival of some Indian women who had been captured at the time of the destruction of the camp, and who were returned to the agency from the Department of the Platte. The women renewed their mourning cries, and among the young men a fresh desire for revenge broke forth.

The next intimation of the affair received at the agency was the return of a successful war party, who had gone down to the outskirts of the Pawnee reservation, and, attacking a herding party, had killed and scalped five Pawnees, returning to the agency without loss to themselves.

Mourning was now turned to joy, and, while the young men joined in the scalp dance, the women trilled their piercing anthems of praise, extolling the bravery of their friends and deriding the cowardly actions of their enemies, as, with the scalps dangling from the ends of long poles, and with wreaths of oak leaves adorning their heads, they marched in procession through the village, chanting as they went.

This blood for blood appeased their resentment, but knowing the vindictive spirit of their enemies, they constantly anticipated a counter attack, and several times the camp was aroused by the report that the Pawnees had been seen on the neighboring bluffs. The young warriors would then mount in hot haste and charge in the direction of the supposed enemy. On one occasion, when such an alarm was spread at evening, a skirmish line was formed outside the village and a brisk fire from their rifles was kept up for some time. When asked why they wasted so much ammunition, they had the poor excuse that they wanted the Pawnees to know that they were on the watch, showing that the Indian's courage needs a little tinkering for the occasion by the medicine man, particularly after dark.

CHAPTER X.

ISSUE OF READY-MADE CLOTHING—TREATMENT OF SAME BY
THE INDIANS—EXPENSIVE EXPERIMENT.

THE first issue of annuity goods made to the
Indians, as has been shown, was entirely
insufficient, the majority of them not receiving
anything ; consequently, I made an effort to
procure more, stating the number of blankets,
yards of Indian cloth, kettles, butcher knives,
buckskin needles and quantity of tobacco,
which would be required to satisfy in part their
desires. Without being consulted in the matter, I was informed that a shipment of ready-
made clothing had been made, that it would
soon arrive at the agency, and that it consisted
of fifteen hundred pairs of pants, the same
number of dress coats, seven hundred great
coats, and one hundred hats.

The Indians had never expressed to me any
desire to change their style of dress ; all of
them, without exception, clung to the fashion
of their forefathers. The half breeds, indeed,
had adopted in part the habit of the whites,

and the white men, who had married squaws, still retained their old dress; but the whole number of these two classes was little more than seventy. Clearly, the supply was too large for them, and, of course, the Department had decreed a grand reform for the wild, unsubdued Sioux. His beaded blanket, in which he took the utmost pride; his ornamented leggins and plain breech cloth, were to be discarded, and he was to be arrayed in attire suitable to his advance in civilization, and thus be better prepared to handle the plough and manipulate those agricultural implements when the spring time came around.

The ready-made clothing arrived. The male portion of the Indians took some interest in the affair, being influenced partly by curiosity and partly by their unswerving desire to be the recipients of anything. The arrangements were much the same as when the other presents were distributed, although, for obvious reasons, the women were undemonstrative, and did not enliven the occasion with their usual chants.

The number of suits of clothing was so great that a decided change in the appearance of the males was naturally expected. But alas for human hopes! I was never able to see its realization. The clothing was originally intended for the defenders of our country, but had been turned aside from its purpose and colored a dark blue, thus making a more stylish citizen dress. An Indian in this costume would be far from poorly attired, although no shirts were provided ; but it did not come up to his ideas, and he proceeded at once to improve upon it. So the legs of the pants were cut off, making rather poor leggins, and the whole upper part discarded. The overcoats were ripped up and appropriated by the women for making skirts. Some of the young bucks did appear in the dress coats, with the skirts and sleeves cut off, thus making a sleeveless jacket, the military buttons being replaced by buttons procured from the trader and fastened upon the impro-vised garment in all directions. The hats were thrown away. Thus this plan of immediate civilization failed; and many good men, who believed that it was not necessary to plod through a generation or two of these people to change their mode of dress to that of their en-lightened benefactors, were doomed to disap-pointment. The experiment cost more than twenty-five thousand dollars, and was for the time perhaps a misdirected expenditure.

CHAPTER XI.

SIOUX AND PONCAS MAKE PEACE—HOW INDIANS MAKE TREA-
TIES WITH EACH OTHER AND BREAK THEM.

WHETSTONE agency was situated in the south-eastern part of the Sioux reserva-tion, and consequently was near to the white settlements in Northern Nebraska and South-ern Dakota; at the same time it was so isolated as to be under none of the constraints of civil-ization.

The Yankton Sioux reservation, upon the opposite side of the Missouri, and some forty miles below, was limited in extent, and its people more or less under the influence of white men. These Indians were supposed to be fast approaching the finishing touches of new-made citizens under the best of religious and secular instructors. Theoretically they were inclined to discard their native dress, and to dispense with the yearly sun dance, and other barbar-ous and sinful practices.

Still further down the river were located the Santee Sioux, still more advanced, for they had actually abandoned their former dress, attended schools and churches, and had among their number many young Indians who had been educated in the East. They were indeed angels compared to what they were a few years before, when, with rifle and bloody knife, they had murdered men, women, and children and destroyed peaceful homes along the western borders of Minnesota.

Both these bands affiliated with the Brulés and Ogallalas, and spoke the same language with only a slight variation, using the D sound, when those west of the Missouri used L, as Dakota and Lakota. They were fond of paying friendly visits to their country cousins at Whetstone, where they could enjoy a reunion, join in the feast, and, throwing off their semi-civilized dress, with nearly naked bodies painted as in the good old days, indulge in the music of the sonorous drum and the wild delights of the scalp dance. Far away from dull teachers and religious instructors, they were once more noble red men.

During the summer and fall of '69, these visits were quite frequent, and were always the occasion for a clamorous demand for additional food, the Indians at the agency representing that the visitors were their friends whom it made their hearts glad to see, and that it would be a breach of hospitality not to be thought of, to neglect to prepare for them a feast. These requests were usually granted, for I knew that they would soon be even with their friends.

The visits were interesting, showing as they did, the true inwardness of these Indians, who were at heart just as much savages as ever, being only glossed over with a thin coating of civilization, and this coating being made possible only because they had been beaten in the field of battle a few years before, imprisoned, and all their leaders ignominiously hung.

The Poncas, speaking a different language from the Sioux, and a remnant of a once powerful band of Indians, allied to the Omahas, occupied a small reservation in the extreme southeast portion of Dakota, west of the Missouri. The Sioux treaty of 1868 wiped out the reservation, but the Poncas still occupied it, being too much reduced in numbers to be thought worthy of much consideration by the Government. The Sioux of Whetstone paid them more or less attention, contending that the Poncas had no right to their reservation, which the Sioux were bound to respect, and so occasionally killed one or more who had ventured too far from their agency buildings, or amused themselves by stealing a few of their ponies at odd times.

The Poncas knew of the visits of the Yanktons and Santees to Whetstone, and so concluded that it would be policy for them also to propitiate these up-country potentates. Accordingly, the principal chief with a few followers came to the agency to reconnoiter, and make complaint as to their treatment, at the same time stating " that they desired above all things to become fast friends of the Sioux, and to live at peace with them in the future." For this purpose he wanted permission to make a visit with a greater number of his followers at an early day, and he asked me to intercede for him with Spotted Tail and other chiefs. The latter proved agreeable to this proposition, and it was finally arranged that the Poncas should come and make the visit without danger to themselves or families.

Upon the appointed day a hundred or more men and women made their appearance, and were welcomed first by the agency Indians, who, of course, had the usual feast procured in the usual way.

After this most interesting ceremony was over, the drums were made to sound, the dance commenced, and the song and wild whoop, common to all tribes, could be heard far into the night.

The next morning there was the council, in which the Sioux at the agency and the Poncas promised eternal fidelity and friendship, and the latter showing with much eloquence how they were cooped up on a small reservation, and were poor and needy; the former made them presents, and led them rejoicing on their way to Spotted Tail's camp. The latter chieftain had made great preparations for a feast, and was ready to receive them with due state. They remained at his camp about two days, and before their return to the agency it was announced there, with much delight, that they had made a lasting peace with Spotted Tail's people.

As they neared the agency on their return, all the Indians there joined in honoring their new-made friends by going out to meet them— the squaws, mounted on their ponies, singing anthems of praise. They all entered the agency in a procession, and there followed in their train a goodly number of ponies—by actual count one hundred and ten, which, together with blankets, robes and trinkets, the Poncas had received as presents from their new allies. Thus these hereditary enemies were, under fortunate circumstances, joined together in the bond of friendship and brotherly love, and the Poncas went home to sleep in peace and security.

According to custom, a few Sioux returned this friendly visit and enjoyed the hospitality of the Poncas, thus having good opportunity to make a friendly inspection of the possessions of the latter.

Before long I was informed, through the agent of the Poncas, that they were losing by theft, not the small Indian ponies given them by the Sioux, but some fine American horses, much prized, and each of more value than many ponies. The Ponca chief visited the agency, reminded his new-made friends of their treaty of peace, and asked for his stolen horses, which had been tracked in that direction ; but, of course, they could not be found. However, more ponies were given in further ratification of friendship. But the Poncas soon lost all their best horses, and when they were gone the ponies followed, until, after a few months, it was generally understood that the compact of eternal fidelity.and friendship had died a natural death, and that the relation of the two tribes of Indians was the same as it had always been.

Not unlike civilized States, where treaties have been consummated for similar causes, and similar results have followed—the stronger taking advantage of the weaker.

Fort Randall, Dakota Territory, looking north, 1860s (courtesy South Dakota State Historical Society)

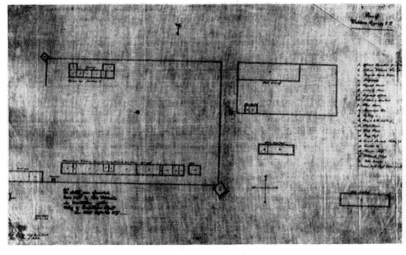

Plan of Whetstone Agency, D.T., 1871 (courtesy South
Dakota State Historical Society)

Spotted Tail, 1872 (photo by Alexander Gardner, Washington, D.C. – courtesy South Dakota State Historical Society)

Blue Horse, 1872 (photo by Alexander Gardner, Washington, D.C. – courtesy South Dakota State Historical Society)

Red Cloud, 1872 (photo by Alexander Gardner, Washington, D.C. – courtesy South Dakota State Historical Society)

The 1870 delegation. Front row: Fast Bear, Spotted Tail, Swift Bear, and Yellow Hair; back row: Charles Gueru and D. C. Poole (from *American Cavalcade* written and privately published by John Hudson Poole in 1939).

CHAPTER XII.

THERE were no school houses or churches at Whetstone, neither teachers nor ministers. My predecessor did ask me to receipt for a school house when receiving the Government property on my arrival, but upon inspection I found that it existed only in imagination. There were a few rough hewn logs collected upon a designated spot of ground, considered an eligible site for a school house, but the structure had not assumed form, except on paper, which would hardly do for the real thing. The trees were still standing from which the church should be built.

The whites engrafted upon the Indians often spoke of their desire for the school, having a hope, perhaps, that the training therein obtained might improve the morals of their half breed progeny, as, indeed, almost any life other than that they were leading would. The Indians only spoke of them incidentally as having been promised them, and anything that had been promised they wanted, whether they could use it or not being a question of no importance. The Department would furnish a teacher when the school house was completed; but, as it provided nothing for building such structure, the teacher was not wanted.

So far as the church and minister were concerned, the Indians were not anxious. They were already provided with a religion of their own, under whose tenets they constantly preached and practiced ; the medicine man being their minister, the blue sky and high bluffs their church edifice. Their religion was one naturally suited to their wants, corresponding to their ideas of morality and their views of justice ; satisfying their longings after immortality, and expressing their views of happiness in the hereafter, and representing their conception of the attributes of the inscrutable and omnipotent Spirit, who rules and governs mankind.

Upon all the more prominent bluffs near the agency could be found evidences of their worship, usually willow sticks five or six feet long, which were set in the ground on the highest elevation, and to which were attached little sacks, made of cloth or dressed skin, containing tobacco, paints, sugar or some little trinket. These were left to sway in the wind and decay, being held sacred from molestation by the Indians, as they were offerings to the Great Spirit. A curiously formed rock or stone found on the prairie was always a shrine of worship, covered with rude figures of wild animals, and with medicine sacks and trifling ornaments hidden in its crevices.

I have seen them at their feasts cast some of their food upon the ground before partaking of it, thus giving to the Great Spirit some portion of each article of food, and then each one in turn asking in an audible voice to be protected and guided in his undertakings. They were constantly propitiating their good spirits, and doing penance to drive away the bad spirits. The young men still practiced cruel tortures to their flesh in the annual sun dance, to fit themselves to endure the hardships and barbarities of the relentless warfare waged against all their enemies.

I saw nothing in their religion but entire selfishness and vindictiveness. They desired even more than ''an eye for an eye and a tooth for a tooth.'' They prayed that their enemies might be utterly destroyed, while they themselves might live and have abundance. The new gospel of peace must be planted in barren ground, indeed, among these people.

They were full of superstition. The flight of birds, the howling of wolves and the barking

of dogs governed their movements. When an
Indian was dying in camp, his male friends remained just outside the lodge, and when the
death was announced discharged their rifles in
the air, thus driving away the evil spirit, Death.
The medicine men practiced upon their imagination to a great extent, not only in preparing
them for the dangers of the battle field, but in
relieving them from bodily pain. On one occasion Blue Horse, an Ogallala brave, exhibited
to me one of the cutting teeth of the beaver,
three or four inches in length. He said, with
the utmost sincerity, that a medicine man had
with much difficulty, a few minutes before, ex-
tracted it from his back, where it had caused
him much pain, but that he was all right now.

Some days before the great eclipse of August,
1869, Dr. C——, physician for the Indians at
the agency, concluded to try his skill as a ma-
gician, and impress the Indians with his magic
art, inseparably connected in their minds with
the healing art.

The doctor announced to some of the principal chiefs and warriors the coming event, telling them the precise time (taken from an al-
manac) when the sun would be obscured and
darkness follow, until he saw fit to have it pass
away. When the day and the hour arrived, the
doctor had his audience in readiness, duly
armed with smoked glass. Being within the

line of totality, and having a cloudless sky and the clear, delightful atmosphere of the plains, the phenomenon was observed under the most favorable circumstances. There was no mistake as to time; the moon gradually crossed the disc of the sun, a black, spherical mass, surely putting out its light.

The Indians were impassive lookers on, until, as the eclipse reached its culmination, leaving only a narrow, bright rim around the outer edge of the sun, the deepening steel-gray shadows attracted their attention, as well as that of beasts and birds. Then, concluding that the exhibition had gone far enough, and that they must drive away the evil spirits, they commenced discharging their rifles in the air. The light of the sun gradually returning, they were thoroughly convinced that it was the result of their efforts, and that the Indians' medicine was better than the white man's.

The doctor could predict the eclipse, but they could drive it away and prevent any evil consequences arising from it. So the doctor failed in fully establishing himself as a big medicine man.

CHAPTER XIII.

INTOXICATING LIQUOR AMONG INDIANS—THEIR USUAL TEM-
PERATE HABITS — THE CHIEF BIG MOUTH RECEIVES HIS
DEATH-WOUND FROM SPOTTED TAIL.

WHETSTONE Agency, although at least fifty
miles from any white settlement, was not
exempt from the baneful influence of the unscrupulous ranchman, who follows in the wake
of our most advanced military posts, and
hovers around secluded Indian agencies, locating as near their boundary lines as possible,
often only a few feet without the jurisdiction of
either. He has, as a squatter sovereign, an eye
for a handsome tract of land, and, at the same
time, locates his ranch on some well-known
road or trail, where he can offer shelter to the
traveler who may pass his way, and dispense
"forty rod" whiskey and other fiery drinks to
the adventurer and desperado, who make his
habitation their headquarters.

Although the general laws as to the sale of
intoxicating liquor upon a reservation were
very strict, and provided severe penalties for

disposing of it to Indians on or off the same, yet, owing to the sentiments favoring this traffic which prevailed among the ranchmen mentioned, detection was well nigh impossible, and conviction of the crime very infrequent. While the laws for the protection of the Indian were ample, could they be executed, a coloring of permission was given by the same power which framed them, by granting to any one, upon the payment of twenty-five dollars, a license to deal in ardent spirits. Armed with such a license, signed by an officer of the Government, the dealer felt justified in vending when and where opportunity offered, unless immediate and forcible means were used to suppress him. These ranchmen usually held such license, and, by clandestine intercourse with half-breeds, carried on a more or less profitable trade with Indians, in this way obtaining their ponies at a low rate, together with furs and peltries, which were taken to white settlements and disposed of.

In my intercourse with Sioux Indians, I found little dissipation among them as a class—very much less than would be found among the same number of white men. There were at the agency a dozen, perhaps, who would become drunk whenever they could find the material, while many of the half-breeds seemed to consider it their bounden duty to indulge at every opportunity, becoming wildly demonstrative, and imitating the gay and festive ranchman and desperado with whom they came in contact, and whom, being white men, they had so often heard praised as enjoying the blessings of civilization.

The chiefs and headmen often denounced the traffic, and Spotted Tail used it constantly as an argument against moving into the agency, saying that he wanted to keep his young men from such temptation. Big Mouth was accused of enjoying strong drink at times, but he never appeared in public when much under its influence. On one occasion he was accused before me of having indulged too freely under the following circumstances:

Some fifteen miles from the reservation, on the east side of the Missouri, was a lonely ranch conveniently located, being equi-distant between Yankton and Whetstone Agency. It was a rude log cabin completely unfurnished, except by a few improvised benches around the fire-place and a barrel of whiskey on tap in one corner, and was kept by the usual style of ranchman, with a Yankton squaw for a wife. This man came to my office one morning, and stated that the night before Big Mouth and a few companions had forced their way into his ranch, driven himself and wife into the brush, helped themselves to his whiskey *ad libitum*, discharged their rifles into the brush where he was

secreted, demolished the door of his cabin,
broken the sash and glass in the window, and
allowed the whiskey to run completely to
waste ; all the time dancing and yelling. He
further stated that he wanted damages, and
fixed the amount at one hundred dollars.
Big Mouth, who was in the office, complacently
smoked while the charges were interpreted to
him, and, as he had no appearance of having
been on a spree, I supposed he would deny it.
On the contrary, he calmly admitted that he
had thus amused himself, but added that, as he
had no money, he could not pay for it.

The ranchman signified his willingness to
take ponies, but Big Mouth was just out of
them, and really could not see what the com-
plainant was going to do about it. He, however, offered him a smoke from his own pipe, a
few whiffs of which was all the ranchman ever
collected. Big Mouth's self-complacency frequently carried him to the verge of facetious-
ness.

His most prominent characteristics, however,
were boastful egotism and arrogance. In his
own estimation he was a mighty chieftain, and
the head of the Ogallala Sioux—a model for
his people and a representative of his race,
whom civilized white men might admire. He
called attention to himself as leading his followers toward changing the manner of their

lives, as the great father desired, and often said that, if he had had all that had been promised him, he and his people would be surrounded by cultivated fields and herds of cattle, and that their wives and children would not want. He would boldly represent in council that, in his desire to cultivate the soil, he had dug up the ground with his fingers, for lack of some better implement, while in truth he was never known to do anything in that direction, except occasionally to listlessly watch his squaws, as they hoed a small patch of corn near by his lodge.

In fact, he was an impracticable and insubordinate leader, whom it had been long in contemplation to depose, by recognizing a better Indian as chief of the loafer band. Having some intimation of this, and feeling that Spotted Tail, chief of the Brulés, was gradually increasing in power and influence, by the number of his followers and the deference paid him when at the agency, Big Mouth manifested his ill feeling and discontent at the tendency to ignore his own importance by trying to disparage Spotted Tail's authority, and boasting that he had only to call upon his relative, Red Cloud, and the latter would seat him firmly in power. This feud continued for some months, being a more or less disturbing element in the management of the Indians at the agency, as was also the more frequent introduction of whiskey, at which Big Mouth, in his ambitious scheme to rule or ruin, connived. A culmination was reached during the night and following morning of October 28th, 1869. Spotted Tail, with some of his warriors, was visiting the agency upon his usual errand. The agency people had been unusually noisy in their nocturnal songs and beating of drums—a pretty sure evidence that whiskey had been introduced.

About daylight I was aroused by a loud knocking at my door, and was excitedly informed by my visitor, the man in charge of the train loaded with supplies for Spotted Tail's camp, that the Indians were fighting, and that they had ordered him not to move out with his train. Upon going outside, I found a brisk discharge of firearms was progressing, the bullets whizzing through the air in various directions and producing an untranquilizing effect.

While I was talking with the teamster, and advising him to go ahead with the train, he suddenly exclaimed, "There they come!" and disappeared. Looking in the direction indicated, I saw two bodies of Indians approaching, fully armed with rifles and revolvers, and with their bows strung; evidently they meant mischief. I was alone, and had not the advantage wished for by the party in a tight place, who only desired some one with a reputation for bravery

to run, and he would try to keep up with him.
As the Indians came nearer, I observed that
they were divided into two parties, one headed
by Spotted Tail, and the other by Blue Horse,
a brother of Big Mouth. Before I could make
up my mind which way to absent myself, I was
surrounded, and, by gestures, directed to go
into the usual council room, which I did, followed by the chiefs and warriors. The situation was awkward and constrained. I did not
know the intentions of the red men, but, as it
had often been intimated that they could kill
all the whites at their leisure and then leave
for parts unknown, I had an uncomfortable
suspicion that the killing was about to commence, and that, for obvious reasons, I should
be the victim, being the only white man present.
Not understanding the language, I could not
tell what they said, should they offer me any
choice as to the manner of my taking off. To
add to the confusion, the discharge of fire arms
continued outside, and every shot might bring
a scalp.

Immediately upon entering the council room,
Blue Horse commenced a furious tirade addressed, as far as I could understand, to the
Brulé warriors. He added to the dramatic
effect by dropping his blanket, and thus ex-
posing his naked form painted for war, a quiver
full of arrows slung to his back, in one hand

his strung bow, and in the other a Winchester
rifle, which lay across the hollow of the arm
holding the bow. A scalping knife and two
navy revolvers strapped to his waist completed
his armament.

In the midst of his wild harangue, as he
bounded about upon the floor gesticulating
fiercely, Spotted Tail, who was seated near me,
quietly reached down under his blanket, unnoticed by Blue Horse, and cocked his rifle.
Evidently now there was to be a desperate
encounter between the two factions, Brulés
and Ogallalas. Confined in a small room, with
all ways of egress stopped by sullen warriors,
each armed with the contents of a small arsenal,
I, a neutral white man, would be the first slain.

This wild scene continued for some time,
when a movement outside indicated an arrival,
and there was ushered into the room a white
man, pale and agitated, whom I knew understood the Sioux language, and could tell me
what was going on.

Blue Horse kept the floor until he gradually
ran down and stopped. I then expected to
hear from the interpreter the fate of the white
men at the agency; that the Indians were tired
of the restraints imposed upon them by the
employés of the Government, and intended to
incontinently murder all of them, help themselves to rations to their heart's content, and

then journey to their friends in the hostile
camps.   But he was given no chance to tell me
the substance of Blue Horse's tirade, for
"Thigh," an Ogallala warrior whom I had
always considered rather inoffensive, rose, and
through the interpreter, addressed some remarks to me.   In the first place, he said, a
large quantity of whiskey had been brought
to the agency, and some of his friends had
taken a little too much.   But who made the
whiskey?   The Indians didn't; but the white
men did.

I had to nod assent to this proposition, and
he continued that, as the white man made
whiskey, and the Indians bought and used it,
it made their hearts bad; and that he was
sorry to say that his friend Big Mouth had
been shot, and now lay dying from the effects
of his wound.   Furthermore, that Spotted Tail
was the man who had committed the act.

So now I had some clue to the unusual
excitement.   Thigh continued his remarks for
some time, denouncing the agency and the
ways of white men generally, but more especially the making of whiskey; closing with a
short eulogy on Big Mouth.   While talking,
he held in his hand a loaded revolver at full
cock, to assist him in his gesticulations and
enforce his points, and as most of the time it
was pointed towards me, and within a few feet

of my head, I was rather glad when he could think of nothing more to say.

Spotted Tail had remained seated from the time of his entrance as unconcerned as a statue, his only movement being the cocking of his rifle when Blue Horse was speaking. He was fresh from the *melee*, but his iron nerves were unshaken. He now rose, and, having first delivered a short temperance lecture. acknowledged that he had shot Big Mouth, excusing his action only so far as to say that he was sorry. He then said that the object of their early visit was to lay the whole matter before me, for me to decide what should be done.

This turn of affairs was calculated to restore my confidence, making me, as it did, a judge in place of victim. I was not particularly sorry that Big Mouth was passing away, but took the poet's license to say that I was; eulogized him as a true friend of his people and of the white man (as I had often heard him say he was), and expressed the hope that they would not allow the matter to go further; for it would be much better to kill their enemies, and not each other who were friends.

This brought forth some "hows" from the braves, and I felt encouraged, and went on to say that, as Spotted Tail had said he was sorry, he would as a matter of course pay Blue Horse, the brother of Big Mouth, some ponies, suggesting ten as about the proper number; and that, as most of them had made a night of it, they had better go to their tepees and sleep, and think over what had been said.

Greatly to my satisfaction they agreed to this proposition, and took their departure.

CHAPTER XIV.

DEATH OF BIG MOUTH.

VERY soon after the departure of the painted savages, who had honored me with this early morning visit, Blue Horse returned, and confided to me that he felt the loss of his noble brother very deeply, and thought that he should be obliged to mourn, meaning to divest himself of paint, arms and ornaments, and show the bereavement usual at the loss of so near a relative. Thinking that it might be the cause of still further demonstration on the part of his friends, I persuaded him by a present of two blankets, which he readily accepted, to delay action until some future day. He then left, and for the first time I had an opportunity to learn the nature of his remarks when on the war path in the council. I found that he had been denouncing Spotted Tail for his murderous act in giving the death-wound to his brother, and had invited him to continue killing Big Mouth's relatives, if he thought best; that he, Blue Horse, was ready and prepared for the conflict when it came his turn.   As intimated, however, his speech, full of pleasant suggestions, produced no particular effect.

Affairs about the agency were far from satisfactory.   The employés were driven from their work by the too close proximity of an occasional bullet, fired from the rifle of some Indian. Some of them, considering discretion the better part of valor, crossed to the opposite side of the Missouri, and found a place of safety. Spotted Tail's supply train was still held in abeyance, the teamsters thinking the risk to their scalps too great to hazard a departure without the consent of the Indians.   The young bucks, dissatisfied with the morning's deliberation, threatened to take matters into their own hands. Being without any adequate means of protection, I dispatched a trusty messenger to Fort Randall, about thirty miles distant, asking for a small detachment of troops and a howitzer to guard the supplies and protect the whites in case matters went from bad to worse.

Big Mouth, though mortally wounded, was still living, and the squaws and medicine men were gathered about him in great numbers, the former shrilly wailing, and the latter beating drums, discharging fire arms, and keeping up a continuous racket.   Although they were familiar enough with wounds to know that their chieftain could not live, word was sent to me that they wanted Dr. C—— to try his healing powers. It was far from a pleasant undertaking to thread our way through this mob of howling savages to the dying Big Mouth.

Upon the approach of the doctor and myself, they made way for us, but redoubled their cries and uproar, whether to give assurance that we would be safe or be scalped we could not tell. We found Big Mouth lying in one corner of a log hut, to which he had been carried after he was shot. The doctor probed the ugly wound in the head of the doughty Ogallala, and convinced himself that he would soon be on his way to the happy hunting ground.

The medicine men and squaws in attendance having closely watched the doctor's examination, and being ignorant of a surgeon's duty, accused him of speeding Big Mouth to his death, thus increasing the danger of our visit.

But fortunately we escaped meeting, on our way back to the agency office, any Indian whose heart had been made bad by this incident. In a short time the death of Big Mouth was announced.

The day, which had commenced with a tragedy, was passed in much uncertainty as to the eventual termination of affairs. When night came I had the employés gathered into an isolated building, which was barricaded as well as possible; and here, supplied with such arms as

could be found, we awaited, with no particular
sense of security, the arrival of the troops,
which very promptly made their appearance at
midnight.

The next morning the presence of troops
served to curb the unruly and suppress the insolent. One white man and two half-breeds, who
had been instrumental in introducing whiskey,
were arrested. Ten or a dozen work oxen were
shot and killed by the Indians during the day,
but order was restored, the troops, with their
prisoners, returned to Fort Randall, and affairs
moved on again as usual.

The dead chief Big Mouth was swathed in
his best blanket, furnished with bow and
quiver, pipe and tobacco, for use in the happy
hunting ground, and duly elevated to a
scaffold to sleep with his fathers. The honor
of filling his place as chief was divided between
Blue Horse and Thigh.

I endeavored to obtain from Spotted Tail an
account of his affair with Big Mouth, but he
would not talk about it, his conduct in this
respect being quite exceptional. Generally
the Indian chief is boastful to a disagreeable
extent. Not so Spotted Tail. He never mentioned himself when it could be avoided, and
would never relate his adventures and bloody
conflicts, which, his friends said, were many.

From the best information of the affair which

I could obtain, Big Mouth was entertaining Spotted Tail on the fatal night, and had, beside the usual feast, some whiskey in his lodge. This he tried to induce Spotted Tail to drink, setting the example himself, but failed. They related stories and sung their Indian songs in company with their respective friends nearly all night, and when, in the early morning, Spotted Tail left the lodge, Big Mouth followed him, and presenting a loaded revolver to his breast, attempted to discharge it; but fortunately the cap failed to explode. Spotted Tail, having had warning of his intentions, was prepared, and sent a ball from his revolver crashing through Big Mouth's brain.

As the latter fell and attempted to rise, two of Spotted Tail's warriors struck him with their revolvers in token of their approval of the act. The friends of both chiefs rallied to their assistance, and had some slight altercation, but did not continue the conflict, marching sullenly instead to the council to eventually accept blood money in place of retribution.

Spotted Tail gave Blue Horse the required number of ponies, and thus Indian laws were vindicated after the manner of our own remote ancestors.

CHAPTER XV.

AMONG the objects of greatest interest to the Indians were the beef cattle kept for issue to them. The cattle for Big Mouth's band were slaughtered and prepared by a professional butcher, and this work always claimed their undivided attention. Mounted upon their ponies they would assist in driving in from the general herd the requisite number of cattle, and remain interested spectators of the killing, having their squaws in attendance to carry home such parts as were rejected by their civilized brother, but by them considered great delicacies.

Fire Thunder and Swift Bear received their beef on the hoof, and their young bucks took a wild delight in treating them like buffalo. They would drive the cattle near to their camps, and, riding at full speed, shoot them with rifles or bows and arrows, according to fancy; thus for the time enjoying the pleasures of the chase. As has been said, Spotted Tail steadily refused to interest himself in transporting to his camp his supplies of bacon, sugar, coffee, etc., but with his cattle it was a different thing. His young warriors were always on hand to receive them, usually from fifty to sixty head at a time, and took pleasure and interest in driving them to their camp, whatever the distance. At this time none but Texas cattle were purchased for the Indians. They were brought from their native prairies, and were wild as any untamed animal. They had the wide, branching horns, long legs and lank bodies peculiar to their breed, seldom weighing, at best, over a thousand pounds gross weight. They were as fleet as an elk, and as easily frightened. The approach of a wolf or a strange dog would often start a whole herd to running, causing a stampede, when it took a good horse and bold rider to overtake them.

But the Mexican herders who had accompanied them from the southern plains were equal to the emergency. One of them riding up to the side of the leader would apply the stinging lash of his long whip to the animal's side, forcing him to sheer off from a direct line, and the rest of the herd following, he soon had them all running in a circle. This was called the "mill," and would be made gradually smaller and smaller, until the

animals impeded each other's further progress, their long horns knocking against each
other in wild confusion, and they finally
stopped, or, in professional language, "were
brought to a round up." Then one would be
allowed to quietly escape in the right direction, and the rest would follow.

At this time traveling on the west side of the
Missouri was not considered safe, especially
for parties with whom the Indians were not
familiar. In consequence of this, the contractors supplying beef cattle to the various
agencies and military posts on the Missouri,
usually crossed their herds to the eastern side
of the river at or below Fort Randall, thus
securing a more frequented route north, and
one comparatively safe. The cattle destined
for Whetstone Agency generally came by this
route, and had to recross the river at the
Agency by swimming. To induce them to do
this was an undertaking attended with many
difficulties. Like most other animals, whether
wild or domestic, they became very much
alarmed when first coming in the vicinity of
wild Indians. A knowledge of this fact is of
great value to the Indians in their stealing
expeditions. Their wild whoop and shaking
of blanket or robe, together with their peculiar
smoky odor, will set the most sober-sided
horse or cow on a perfect rampage.

When a herd was to be crossed at Whetstone, the usual proceeding was to find a bold bluff, intersected by a wide ravine which led to the water's edge. The herders would drive the cattle to the head of this ravine and start them gently toward the river, increasing their speed until, as they were about entering the stream, the leaders were at a full run. They would then be plunged into the swift current by their own inertia and by their followers closely packed in their rear. The opposite bank would be kept clear of Indians, and often a few staid work oxen placed near its edge as decoys; while on the shore from which the cattle were starting, mounted men would be stationed who, by shouting and discharging fire arms, would try to keep the animals moving in a line to the opposite bank.

A few feet from the first plunge into the water the cattle would be swimming, breasting the rapid current, but the leaders, getting a first whiff of the tainted Indian air from the agency, would invariably turn their course and swim back toward the bank which they had just left. In spite of the screaming of those on shore, the sharp cracking of whips and the discharging of fire arms, the half-crazed leaders would blindly return, and, coursing along the bank to a second ravine, dash through it and out on to the prairie, followed, into the river and out again, by the whole herd of five or six hundred.

After a long chase the herd would be "rounded to," and driven to the head of the ravine to repeat the same manœuver. This was often done again and again, in the hope each time that some animal would conclude to cross to the opposite shore, and thus set an example which the others would surely follow.

In the fall and spring, when the water was cold, which added to the difficulty, I have spent three or four days in trying to "make a crossing," as it is called, being assisted by the practical lore of the professional herder, the knowledge of the frontiersman, and by the Indians, who were the most expert of all. Any one of the last would ride boldly into the water among the struggling animals, and swimming his pony to the side of one of the leaders, jump astride his back, and try to keep him in a direct course for the opposite bank by knocking with a club on his long horns when he attempted to turn, which he generally did. When fairly on the way to the shore, and beyond the possibility of turning, the Indian would draw his pony to his side by his long lariat, remount and extricate himself from the swimming mass of infuriated animals. The white men following on the flanks, and swimming their horses into the water, would come to the shore shaking with cold, while the Indians and half-breeds would be unaffected, although naked except the kilts about their loins.

After many and various attempts at crossing, the same herd would be brought to the river, driven in, and, without any apparent cause, would strike out for the opposite shore, seemingly thinking further opposition useless.

The forcible manner of driving would sometimes be varied, after a day's rest, by taking advantage of one of the peculiarities of these animals. A herder would ride out in front of them, and by singing in a low voice a melodious song, or whistling in a minor key, he could often lead the whole herd in any direction he wished, apparently charming them by his really musical notes.

The waters of the Missouri, with their ever varying channel, like the ghost in "Hamlet," "now here, now there," rendered the finding of a landing for a steamboat a matter of experiment, and it was often necessary to land stores two or three miles from the agency. The Indians always found their way to the temporary landings, and, seating themselves on prominent points of observation, were seemingly passive lookers on, but really they were intensely interested as to the number of bales of blankets, boxes of tobacco, barrels of sugar and sacks of coffee.

Handling these supplies and hauling them to shelter from threatening storms were often questions of great moment, but under no circumstances was I ever able to get the Indians to assist in this labor. My own example passed for nothing. This was to them hewing of wood and drawing of water, and, according to the laws of their customs, women's work, far beneath their dignity as lords of creation.

The Sioux are not indolent and lazy after the manner of Hottentots, for, when called upon to perform what they consider man's work, they exhibit remarkable endurance and activity. Unequaled in the hunt and chase, when providing for their families; unsurpassed in horsemanship; bold scouts and faithful couriers; masters of their various weapons; fitted to endure the winter's cold and summer's heat; and fully partaking of the characteristics of all born to the rigors of a northern climate, their energy, if properly directed, would carry them into much more useful and surer fields of advancement than does the policy in their treatment heretofore indicated.

Why endeavor to make of poor material unwilling agriculturists, in place of leading them to a pastoral life, for which they show considerable inclination, and which has always come first in the regular state of advancement from barbarism to civilization?

CHAPTER XVI.

DISTINGUISHED CHIEFS ARRIVE AT THE AGENCY FOR THE
WINTER—PAWNEE KILLER AND BUCK—SURVEYING PARTY
—INDIANS AND INDIANS.

THE routine of affairs at the agency during
the winter was occasionally relieved by
the arrival of some distinguished chieftain,
with a more or less numerous following, who
had passed the summer and fall in raiding on
stock and taking scalps in the direction of the
Platte River, or with congenial friends in the
Powder River country, or the Rose Bud, and,
now that cold weather had come, visited the
agency to spy out the land, and see how it
fared with their brethren who were making
pretensions to "learn the ways of white men,"
as the Indians expressed it.

One of these chiefs was Red Leaf. He had
the reputation of being a bold warrior and gallant leader, and of having taken a leading part
in the Fort Phil. Kearney massacre of 1866.

Red Leaf's followers, men, women and children, had a much wilder appearance than their

friends at the agency. In place of woolen blankets and calico dresses, indicative of contact with an agency and annuity goods, they wore gaily painted and ornamented robes, buckskin leggins, and garments made of dressed deer and antelope skins, decorated with beads and bright-colored porcupine quills. This dress, corresponding to their wild habits, added much to their novelty and picturesqueness.

Their presence carried with it the impress of their wild, native independence. Their manner had more of ease and confidence, their step was more elastic and firm, and their eyes more keen in the quick glance of observation, than the agency Indians. Beside them the latter appeared to be in a stage of semi-somnambulism, from over-feeding and want of exercise. They were in the torpor of the chrysalis state, waiting to come forth, under the peace policy, full fledged white men in manners and habits. At present the wilder sons of the prairie had the advantage in point of appearance.

If they were thus attractive to me, it was not strange that their own kith and kin should be still more interested in them, and should show them, still true representatives of their race, every mark of admiration and esteem.

Their coming was always announced days beforehand by Indian couriers, who were constantly carrying news from camp to camp, and their arrival waited for with impatience. The agency Indians killed the fatted calf and sung and danced before them, and in their zeal to help their friends made inordinate demands for blankets, tobacco, powder and lead—the coveted wants of all Indians. As I had none of these articles in store, they could not be supplied, and the next demand would be for a large quantity of food. The latter was given, after assurance by the new comer that it was his present intention to locate near the agency, or with Spotted Tail, and, as a matter of course, remain at peace.

Another visitor was Roman Nose, a Minneconjou Sioux, celebrated among the Indians as the active leader in many bold forays against their enemies. He, with a number of lodges, made his appearance when snow began to fly, and wanted rations and quiet for the winter under the usual promise.

Roman Nose wore at this time a hunting jacket made of dressed skins, which was trimmed about the neck and shoulders with scalp locks taken from those he had killed. The hair was long and much too fine for that of Indians. Some poor white women had paid the penalty of following their husbands into the sparsely settled parts of Kansas and Nebraska, thus encroaching on the hunting ground of this noble savage.

Whistler, an Ogallala, who had made himself rather notorious during the summer months on the Republican and Platte Rivers, turned his course towards Spotted Tail's camp, causing the latter to ask for an increased supply of cattle, bacon, etc.

And last, though not least, Pawnee Killer, an Ogallala brave, made his appearance at the agency with a small following. This chieftain was well known on the Republican, and at Forts Laramie and Fetterman. He announced that he had been operating in the field with a small force during the summer, and implied that he had come to the agency for rest and recreation for the winter.

So far as villainy can be depicted in the human countenance, it was to be found in Pawnee Killer's. His face had a lean and hungry look; he was long and lank, and reminded one of a prowling wolf. He seldom smiled while talking with his companions, but stalked about with his blanket closely wrapped around him, as if expecting at each turn to pounce upon an enemy, or be himself attacked. He had a murderous looking set of followers, and all indications pointed to the fact that they had come red handed from killing an innocent party of white men on the Republican River, in Nebraska. During the month of August, 1869, Mr. Nelson Buck, in charge of a survey-

ing party, consisting of twelve persons, was
making surveys of Government land in Nebraska, when the party was attacked by Indians and all of them killed. Pawnee Killer
and his friends were supposed to have been engaged in the affair, and to know the particulars, which the friends of Mr. Buck and others
were anxious to obtain, as also their bodies for
decent burial. It was made my duty to investigate the matter.

Through the influence of a supply of rations
and a gift of tobacco, Pawnee Killer was induced to relate this version of the affair, which
was corroborated by his friends. That he,
with a number of other Indians, while hunting
on the Republican, in Nebraska, during the
past summer, had discovered a party of surveyors engaged at work, and near by their
temporary camp, in which were tents and a
wagon, which the Indians supposed contained
provisions. A man was engaged cooking at a
camp fire near the wagon, and some of the
young men of Pawnee Killer's party approached him with the intention of asking for
food, as they were hungry. While they were
asking for something to eat, some of the surveying party approached, and, while partially
concealed in a clump of brush, fired upon them,
wounding one of the Indians.

This commenced the fight in which eight, of

the party of twelve, surveyors were killed,
while the Indians lost three killed. Four of
Mr. Buck's party, who had entrenched themselves, they were unable to dislodge, so, after
destroying the camp and wagon and such
surveying instruments as they could find, they
retired from the scene of conflict. The remaining four. surveyors, Pawnee Killer supposed were killed by another party of Indians
known to be near there.

Pawnee Killer excused the act on the ground
that the white men commenced the fight, and
enraged his young men so that he could not
restrain them. This was all the information I
could gain. There was no further proof that
he himself was one of the murderers of the
Buck party, but I never thought he was any
too good to be.

I found that there were Indians and Indians.
But many people living at a distance judge
them as all one class. When reading accounts
of the cruel brutality with which some of the
murders of white men are committed, they
jump to the conclusion that all Indians, wherever found, are murderers, and should be
exterminated. This judgment, I believe,would
not be given upon a more intimate acquaintance with these people, for there are undoubtedly many among them who have never committed outrages except in a state of war, and

then, under their tribal system, all must become involved as a matter of self-preservation.

We must remember the brutal outrages committed every day by white men in civilized communities. This universal condemnation of an unenlightened people has resulted in great injustice to them. Indians have been mercilessly shot down simply because they were Indians.

When this indiscriminate condemnation is so common among civilized people, it is not strange to find it almost universal with the savage. If an Indian is enraged by a real or supposed injury from a white man, he swears vengeance on the whole race, and one white man's scalp is as good as another.

CHAPTER XVII.

DISCONTENT—EPXEDITIONS TO EXPLORE THE BLACK HILLS
AND WOLF MOUNTAINS.

DURING the fall of 1869 and winter of 1870, more than usual discontent appeared among the Indians, due to various causes, one of the principal of which was the lack of suitable clothing and shelter in the severe winter weather of that latitude. Their tepees were thin and worn, and no canvas had arrived to renew them, while the distribution of ready-made clothing had been anything but satisfactory. They had no idea of exchanging their native dress for the cheap clothing of soldiers, dyed to conceal its original design. The goods suitable to their wants, for which I had asked so long ago, had not arrived, and I was obliged to listen to many uncomplimentary remarks regarding my efficiency as an agent, and even some reflections on my character for truthfulness.

The wild and turbulent spirits which the approach of winter had brought among them

helped to increase the discontent and dissatis-
faction by their accounts of the bold raids, the
startling attacks upon their enemies and the
pleasures of the chase, which they had enjoyed
during their free and independent summer life.
The old habits never lost their charm, and
beside them their present life seemed tame and
dull.

The ranchman became more bold in his nefarious trade, owing to the failure to convict in
the courts some of the most notorious venders
of intoxicating drink.   In spite of the best pre-
cautions possible under the circumstances,
there was considerable whiskey consumed at
the agency, greatly to the detriment of the
Indians and their associates.

They were still smarting under the chastise-
ment of their friends by the Pawnee Scouts,
and the young men meditated further vengeance.

They had again asked permission to hunt on
the Republican, under the stipulations of their
treaty, and to be accompanied by some reliable
white man, who should govern their movements
and see that they did not molest settlers.   This
request had been refused, and, considering
that an injustice had been done them, they
constantly referred to the subject in their
talks.   It was indeed a serious matter to them,
for the buffalo is a perfect store house of family

supplies. His robe more than takes the place of the white man's blanket; his dressed and smoked hide make better material for lodges than canvas ; the rich marrow of his bones furnishes butter; his dried sinews their thread; his hoofs and horns the glue to strengthen and embellish their bows and complete their arrows; while his flesh is their natural food the year round, that which is not wanted for immediate use being dried without salt in the pure air of the plains and preserved for future use.

Another grievance was that they learned, through the whites engrafted on them, of meetings in eastern cities which were addressed by speakers giving glowing accounts of the richness of the country which the Sioux occupied. These individuals drew entirely upon their imagination for these facts, exaggerating in proportion to their ignorance of the real resources of the country. They pictured a new Eldorado in the Big Horn Mountains and Black Hills, and called upon the adventurers and enterprising to join expeditions which were to start in the spring from Laramie in the south, and from some point in Montana in the north-west, and fight their way through to their destination in spite of hostile Indians.

The Northern Pacific Railroad was projected, and newspapers gave glowing accounts of the rich lands west of the Missouri to be opened

to the agriculturist, and of the beds of coal
and mines of gold and silver. These matters
were discussed in meetings and by newspapers
without the slightest reference to the rights
and possessions of the Indians guaranteed by
solemn treaty. The same unsettled state of
affairs as at Whetstone extended to all the
agencies on the Missouri. The Indians became
more and more clamorous and demonstrative,
and I determined to ask for a small detachment
of troops to be permanently stationed at the
agency. I required some adequate means to
arrest white offenders against the intercourse
laws, as well as to curb the Indians.

The young bucks did not look with favor
upon the arrival of troops. Naturally enough
they did not wish to be restrained in the least,
but it seemed likely to prove good discipline
for them. The elder and more conservative
Indians looked upon the matter with indifference.

So the guard of troops arrived, and some
months later a permanent garrison was established, and had a beneficial effect.

CHAPTER XVIII.

THERE had been several Dakota blizzards during the winter. These storms are peculiar to the plains; the air is filled with fine particles of sharp, cutting ice and snow, which are driven and whirled with blinding force by a gale of wind, often obscuring the sun and even objects but a few feet distant, the mercury at the same time standing many degrees below zero.

The Indians have learned to remain in their lodges during these storms, or, if traveling, to move with their families and ponies into some sheltered ravine, and there await the subsidence of the gale; but the inexperienced traveler, who endeavors to keep on his journey, is blinded by the fury of the blast, loses his way, and often perishes of cold and hunger.

These storms usually last three days, and then the wind dies down to a gentle breeze, the sun shines out warm and clear in a cloudless sky, and those who live in the land can come forth and look over their losses of cattle and horses, buried in snow drifts and dead from suffocation and cold, if not to mourn the loss of some too adventurous friend, who has perished by the way side.

Under many difficulties a fence had been built around one of the principal cultivated fields at the agency. The trees had been felled and the logs hauled to the saw mill, where they were made into fence boards; cedar posts had been rafted from an island in the river above the agency; and the whole, when finished, was looked upon with much pride by the head farmer, as being a mile and a half of good board fence, as it was. I had repeatedly called the attention of the Indians to it, and asked them to watch over it and see that it was not injured, as, when spring came, it would be wanted to protect the corn and grain which were to be cultivated. During one of these blizzards of the highest type, there were four days during which none of the agency employés ventured out, and when they did it was to discover that the much admired board fence had almost entirely disappeared. The squaws had appropriated boards and posts, and cut them up for their lodge fires. The men must have been aware of it, but, as the squaws ordinarily had to pack all their wood on their backs from an island half a mile or more distant, they probably winked at the depredation, and, when they saw the fence boards brought in and piled upon the blazing fire, took the chances of having another fence built of green cottonwood boards, which would be dry enough for tepee fires next winter. I took the first occasion to speak of the loss of the fence, but they failed to shed tears or feel deeply depressed at the rather expensive way their squaws had taken to keep them comfortable during the storm.

In February there appeared a train of wagons from below, loaded with the long-expected blankets, etc. The delay in their arrival diminished greatly the effect of the beneficence. Over six months of waiting from day to day would destroy the heart of a more patient people.

These goods were among the first purchased under the supervision of the peace commissioners, and the blankets and cloths were all of the best quality. The quantity was large, and supplied all with articles which they had long needed. Thirty-one thousand yards of canvas gave them new lodges, eight hundred blankets gave one to each warrior, seventeen thousand yards of calico gratified female wants and vanities, and fifty boxes of tobacco solaced chiefs and warriors as they smoked and meditated. For the time their hearts were glad. I improved the opportunity to remind them of the desire of their Great Father that they should learn to cultivate the soil. They made the usual promise, and said that they were perfectly willing to do so provided they had the means. All they wanted was plenty of hoes and seed corn; I should see. But this talk I had already discovered amounted to nothing so far as they were individually concerned, as each particular talker in council (the women were never allowed even to listen) meant, when expressing a willingness to work, that he would put his squaws at it, and nothing more. I never saw but one Indian man working in the field while at this agency. He was old and superannuated, and had lost all regard for the pomps and vanities of this world.

Swift Bear had received a good number of blankets and a quantity of tepee cloth, and was inclined to be rather eloquent on the subject of agriculture. He even went so far as to say that he wanted a ploughed field to himself, with a good house near at hand, where he could sit and watch his corn and potatoes growing, while his people could look on, admire, and perhaps imitate his example.

I took him at his word. A few acres were broken and fenced about on a spot selected by himself, and a comfortable log house erected as he desired. But it never pleased him. He

was no better than the rest, and turned his
squaws out to labor, while he made use of his
house only by moving his canvas tepee near it.
Thus he realized his dreams of being a husband-
man.

CHAPTER XIX.

SPOTTED TAIL AS A FARMER—HIS CAMP AT A DISTANCE
FROM THE AGENCY—ITS CONTENTMENT AWAY FROM CIVIL-
IZING INFLUENCES.

WHILE he was visiting at the agency, Spotted
Tail was approached on the important subject of settling down and cultivating the soil.
He was offered plenty of ploughed ground, a
good log house, and all the farming implements
he wanted, but he either evaded the subject
altogether or declined the offers, on the ground
that he did not like the situation at the present
agency, nor, in fact, any other point upon the
Missouri. He wanted an agency located upon
the White Earth River, or at almost any point
except the present one. While talking to him
on the subject of farming, he seemed to take
about as much real interest in the matter as a
well-to-do farmer would were he asked to adopt
the habits and fashions of a Sioux Indian. It
was the same with most of the Indians under
his control. They often compared their manner of living very favorably with that of the

white men with whom they came in contact, whose manners and customs they could not see were any improvement upon their own. In many instances they were not far out of the way.

There were, as has been mentioned, a number of white men at the agency who had married Sioux women, but at this time none of them dwelt in Spotted Tail's camp. I knew but one white man that did. He was a hard-looking specimen, much more untidy in appearance than the Indians with whom he lived. I never learned where they picked him up, but he was seemingly contented with his lot, though he was simply tolerated among them, and treated as a menial, being required to bring wood and water and fetch coals of fire to light their pipes.

This man had some education, and I tried to employ him, as he lived in their camp, to give me some information as to the number of people in the village—a subject guarded by them with jealous care. But either from indolence or from fear of the Indians he was never of any assistance, and I soon dropped him.

Spotted Tail and those associated with him were much interested in the arrival of the annuity goods, and, in order to have them quickly delivered at their camp—and also to supply themselves with tepee poles, the frame work of their dwellings, moved their camp to within twenty-five miles of the agency. The new camp was toward the northwest, and near the Missouri, so that they were but a short distance from an island, upon which was a small growth of cedar of proper size for the squaws to make into tepee poles. As each tepee required about fifteen poles to pitch it properly, and as from constant use they often became broken and unserviceable, this was a matter of great importance. The new blankets having been donned, and the new canvas made into tepees, Spotted Tail was inclined to be proud of these acquisitions, and invited me to visit his camp and see how comfortably he and his people were living. As their new outfit had been obtained principally through his persistent exertions, he claimed rightfully the honor it brought with it.

Accordingly, one bright spring morning, I set out for the Indian village, accompanied by my interpreter. By following a well defined trail, made by the trains which transported supplies, and by the passage of moving families with packed ponies, and tepee poles trailing on the ground, we had no difficulty in finding our way over the otherwise level and trackless prairie.

As we approached the village, we found a more broken country, our trail leading over high buttes and across deep ravines. Making a few short turns at the base of the buttes, and ascending the side of a ravine, we came in view of the camp. Scattered in rather irregular order were about three hundred and fifty lodges. An open space in the centre answered the purpose of a public square, and overlooking this was the council lodge, and, in close proximity to it, Spotted Tail's tepees, three in number. We were escorted to one of these, and as we approached he emerged and welcomed us, inviting us to dismount and enter. Upon doing so we were immediately offered coffee and meat to refresh us after our morning ride. My interpreter had warned me that feasting would be the principal entertainment, so I governed myself accordingly and did not partake too freely the first time.

Like other great rulers, Spotted Tail had his little annoyances, known only to those behind the throne. Being the principal chieftain, he was constantly called upon by those wanting counsel and advice, and custom demanded that all callers should have something offered them to eat, so that his larder had constant drafts made upon it. In order to sustain his dignity in this respect, I sent him extra coffee, bacon and sugar by each supply train, the articles being left without comment in his lodge. This was in addition to his regular share. On this very day there were no less than five or six warriors in the lodge, who were replenishing themselves from the boiling pot suspended over the fire.

The interior of the tepee showed no marks of princely state, or tokens of power and wealth. It was of ordinary size, of the well-known conical shape of all Sioux Indian lodges, and so filled in around the edge with family stores of various kinds that but little room was left for the occupants. In the center was the fire, the smoke from which escaped through a hole in the top, and around it were robes and blankets spread upon the ground. On these you could lounge with your back against the stores, and your feet at a comfortable distance from the fire. The smoke of the Indian tobacco (composed of one-third tobacco and two-thirds of the inner bark of the red willow, dried), together with a portion of the smoke from the fire, usually fills the upper part of a tepee, and gives its contents a not unpleasant smoky odor.

Spotted Tail's favorite wife was doing the honors. It was said that he possessed three others, but he did not take sufficient pride in them to have them call around on this occasion.

Going outside and looking around the village, I found everywhere an air of quiet contentment. It was situated in a sheltered place, and the rays of the spring sun were warm, so most of the Indians were out of doors ; the elder ones smoking as they basked in the sun, the young bucks, divided into two parties, enjoying their favorite game of foot ball, and

the boys whipping tops or practicing with their
bows and arrows.   The women were working
and gossiping, always at a distance from the
men, and the girls too small to carry burdens
were playing with their rude dolls or acquiring
knowledge of the needle with dried sinews
for thread.   Some of the young maidens, I
noticed, lingered a little as they carried wood
and water, casting shy glances on the young
athletes running after the ball.   In the distance
herds of ponies grazed on the prairie, watched
by sentinels posted on high buttes to see that
they did not stray too far, and to give timely
warning should an enemy approach.

The whole was a pleasant scene of primitive
life.   Here was a community ruled by chiefs
and sub-chiefs who had gained their positions
by their bravery in battle and discretion in
council, and who maintained them partly by
their prowess and partly by a certain acquies-
cence in the wishes of the majority.   If simple
contentment be the aim of life, why should
they be made "to sweat and groan under a
weary load ?"

Upon further investigation I found that the
camp was conveniently located for wood and
water.   Being new it was cleanly, and the
white canvas contrasted finely with the fresh
unbroken green sward of the prairie.   For a
summer camp it was finely situated.   Their

previous camp, from which they had just moved, had been very differently located in a secluded valley, where it was sheltered from the biting winter wind by the surrounding bluffs, and with plenty of dry wood at hand for fires, and also green cotton wood limbs, whose succulent bark forms the only food for their ponies when deep snows cover the ground.

After looking about the village for some time we proceeded to the council lodge, which had floating from its peak an empty flour sack. Upon inquiry I found that this was intended for the Stars and Stripes, and was referred to as such by the speakers in the talk which followed. Upon entering the lodge we found the chiefs and warriors awaiting us. The most noted of them were Spotted Tail, Two Strike and Red Leaf of the Brulés, and Black Bear, Whistler and Pawnee Killer of the Ogallalas.

They had made a little more than the usual feast, and in my honor had killed the fatted calf and prepared a dainty dish much relished by themselves. One of their customs requires that a guest must eat of each dish that is set before him, and the entire amount to which he is helped, otherwise an implied slight is cast upon the repast, and a present must be given to the host. The morning ride in the bracing air had fortunately fortified me with a good appetite and keen relish for almost anything in the shape of wholesome food. The coffee was served, and a big kettle brought in and placed where all could see when its savory contents should be disclosed. This interesting moment had arrived, and one of the warriors, using a stout stick for a fork, ran it into the steaming kettle and drew forth—a good-sized dog ! It had been denuded of its hair, and parts of its legs were gone, but that there should be no doubt about it, as is the custom with our fine cooks when placing before us some rare bird or fish, the head and tail were left on the body entire.

I took my share and with many misgivings tried to eat some of it. It really tasted about the same as young pig, but to me " the scent of the roses clung to it still," and I willingly paid the forfeit which some of the warriors soon claimed. The Indians all partook with the utmost gusto and relish. The talk which followed did not elicit much that was new. While they were satisfied with the last distribution of annuity goods, they still indicated their uneasiness for want of assurances, which I could not give, that they would remain undisturbed in their present possessions. They still desired to hunt buffalo, and did not consider that they were sufficiently revenged upon the Pawnees.

Though Spotted Tail brought these matters in review, he announced, in the presence of all, his intention to remain at peace, and to urge his young men to do the same.

Two Strike, an active leader among the warriors, intimated that as every effort had been made to gain permission to hunt in the Republican River country, and without success, it was possible they might go without it. He again referred to the killing of their friends there, and spoke in no very complimentary terms of the Pawnee Scouts and of the Government which employed them.

The other chiefs contented themselves with applauding such parts of Spotted Tail's and Two Strike's remarks as coincided with their views. The council over, I was invited to visit the tepees of the other chiefs.

Upon entering each one, some food was offered, but, after the dog feast, I constantly made myself liable to the customary penalty for not eating what was set before me.

These visits over, and after the usual hand shakings and "hows," I remounted and with my interpreter rode briskly back to the agency. I enjoyed the visit, affording, as it did, the opportunity to see the Indians at home and undisturbed by the presence of white men, whose customs and manners are so widely at variance with their own.

CHAPTER XX.

WINTER — HOW PASSED — YOUNG INDIANS DREAMING OF
SCALPS AND STEALING HORSES — NO TASTE FOR FARM-
ING.

THE winter had been spent in listening to the
complaints of the Indians upon nearly
every subject connected with their manner of
life; in looking after the stores for issue, Capt.
Woodson, Acting Commissary, having been relieved and sent to other fields of duty; in hearing complaints of white men who came to the
agency from the white settlements in Nebraska,
looking for stolen horses, as they said, but who
had all the appearance of a class who are not
averse to taking a hand at stealing an unpro-
tected horse themselves; in hearing recitals of
depredations by Indians against white men,
and of white men against Indians, and en-
deavoring to adjust their differences; called
upon frequently to attend a night council in an
unfrequented lodge, gotten up by some schem-
ing warrior who had an enterprise on foot,
which, should he succeed in having it carried

out, might add to his importance when brought
before the general public.

The northern spring was welcomed with more
than usual delight, affording, as it did, an opportunity to escape indoor work, and to visit
the fields, which, theoretically, were to bud
and blossom under the cultivation of the Indians. The interest taken in agriculture by the
chiefs was, as heretofore explained, a minus
quantity, but then others, not holding exalted
positions, might be induced to go into the fields
if a proper example were shown them, and commence the long road marked out for their advancement.

Great efforts were made, with the limited appliances at hand, to rebuild the fence destroyed
by the squaws in the winter. All the work oxen
that had not been maliciously killed were yoked
to ploughs to break up new ground; horses
were harnessed to cross ploughs, and the old
fields prepared for seeding and planting. This
preparatory work was attended to with interest
and alacrity by the employés. The Indians
were invited to watch the work as it progressed,
and to go with me while I held a plough or drove
a team; but the force of example was still a
failure. The squaws again came to the rescue,
and when the time came worked diligently in
their rude way, while the men smoked and
dreamed, and some lamented that they were

too old to change their ways for those of white men. Instead of the brown, dried grass or the black surface of the burnt prairie, fresh green covered bluffs and buttes and valleys, and the young bucks, who dreamed of glory and renown and future chieftainships, were stirred to action as usual at this time of year. There were horses to be stolen and scalps to be taken, and they knew where to find them. Mounted on their ponies, completely armed and with a small amount of provision tied to their saddles, leading their best war horses to be mounted only at the critical moment, they were prepared for any journey. Some secluded valley, with its running brook and willow-covered banks, would afford them shelter and rich pasturage for their hardy animals after a day or night of travel. Should success crown their efforts they were sure of a welcome when they returned; their names and their deeds would be remembered in the songs of the women; they could shout their exploits in the scalp dance, and wear their new-made honors in council.

To settle down and quietly cultivate the soil was farthest from their thoughts.

In the midst of the spring work word came to me one day that Spotted Tail and two hundred warriors were on their way to the Pawnee reservation, in Nebraska. At the same time it

was stated that he was led to this by the refusal
of his young men to take his advice and remain
at home; as he could not stop them, he would
lead them to see that they did not molest white
men.

The chief had been at the agency on the same
day on which the information was given as to
his contemplated movement, but had not, according to custom, called upon me, and had
taken his departure very suddenly for the purpose stated.

Ponca Creek takes its rise in a northwesterly
direction, and in its course south runs some
twenty-five miles back from the agency, parallel
to the Missouri; then, tending towards the
southeast, joins the Niobrara River. It is a
beautiful, clear, pebbly-bottomed stream, with
a sparse growth of wood here and there upon
its banks. An Indian trail had long run near
its course, made by the hostile Sioux on their
raids toward the south, and my informant indicated a point on the creek where Spotted Tail
and his people would camp for the night.
After having notified the Superintendent of
Indian Affairs of the supposed movement of
the Indians, I started with a half-breed interpreter for the place, a ride of about thirty
miles, hoping to meet Spotted Tail, if he were
really on the war path, and to persuade him
and his followers to return.

On arriving at Ponca Creek, much to our surprise we found no signs of the war party. Shortly after we were joined by two Indians from Spotted Tail's camp, but the interpreter could gain no information from them. They did not appear to enjoy our company, but evidently had no intention of leaving us. I had brought a small lunch to share with my interpreter. Our new-found guests came in for a very large half, so the original party did not suffer from indigestion.

Near sun-down a furious rain storm set in, and the night becoming so dark that we could not retrace our trail to the agency, we had to resort to a "wick-i-up," made with willow sticks and our saddle blankets. Our new friends were not backward, and crawled in with us. I have passed more comfortable nights than the one watching war parties on the banks of Ponca Creek.

I found out afterward that our uninvited guests were watching my movements.

The next morning I returned, with my interpreter, cold and hungry, to the agency, to learn that Spotted Tail was in his camp. Some of his young men had gone south in spite of his remonstrances, but my expedition was entirely too late.

The following letter, received in consequence of their running forays, shows by implication

that the agent was held responsible for the conduct of the Indians under his charge and supposed to be under his control. The good man
who wrote it evidently had implicit faith that
the Pawnees did not go upon the war path, and
thought that their scouts after stray camps of
Sioux, hunting buffalo on the Republican, were
not a cause of irritation to the former. The
Pawnee scouts, it is true, were fighting under
the United States flag and by order of the Government, but the Sioux could not understand
this distinction, and considered the assault as
coming from their hereditary enemies, and to
be revenged accordingly:

PAWNEE AGENCY,
GENOA, NEBRASKA.

To the Agent at Whetstone Agency.

MY FRIEND: I write to inform you that a
party of Indians, supposed to belong to your
agency, and variously estimated from one hundred and fifty to two hundred, made a raid
upon the Pawnees early on the morning of the
6th instant, killing three Indian women. They
were pursued by the Pawnees and United States
soldiers, under Captain Egan, and one of their
number killed. These raids are quite frequent,
and always made up in part with Indians of
your agency. I was informed by a white man,
who says he was at your agency about the time
the last raiders previous to these returned, that

the particulars of the raid were generally known there. I then wrote to the agent in regard to it, but never received an answer.

I use every effort in my power to prevent the Pawnees from making raids upon other agencies, and when they have I require them to return the ponies stolen. No complaint has been made to me of any Indians being killed by the Pawnees except in resisting these raids, whilst nine Indians have been killed by the Sioux since I took charge of them on the 1st of 6th mo., 1869.

Very respectfully,

* * * *

Indian Agent.

CHAPTER XXI.

RUMORS OF DISCONTENT AMONG SIOUX INDIANS—SPOTTED
TAIL AND OTHERS INVITED TO WASHINGTON BY THE
PRESIDENT.

AS the season advanced, increasing rumors of
hostilities prevailed throughout the Sioux
country, and various communications were received upon the subject.   One, from the con-
sulate at Winnipeg, in a British province, stated
that five hundred well-armed and clothed warriors had started thence on the war path for the
Missouri River.   Others from Fort Buford, in
the northwest, gave warning that signal fires
had been lighted on the prairies, and that a
council was to be held in June to unite the
hostile bands in an effort to drive the whites
from the Missouri River.   Two additional regiments of infantry were distributed at various
military stations and Indian agencies on the
river.   At Whetstone there was no apparent
change in the disposition of the Indians other
than a general uneasiness for reasons that have
been stated.   I was called upon by the authori

ties more frequently for reports as to the future
designs of the Indians, so far as they could be
understood, and ordered to give timely warning
of any movements.   I was also told to again
admonish the Indians that they must not go
south towards Kansas and the Union Pacific
Railroad, and that should they be found there
they would be driven back by soldiers, and
that hunting on the Republican would be upon
dangerous and forbidden ground.

While engaged in carrying out these instructions, I received an order from the President to
come without delay to Washington, bringing
with me Spotted Tail, Swift Bear, two principal
warriors, and an interpreter.   As this promised
a change, I was prepared to obey the order with
alacrity.   I was glad to be relieved from the
disagreeable duty of choosing the chiefs who
should be honored with an opportunity to visit
their Great Father, whose name they had so
many times used in council, but I must make
selection of the two warriors and an interpreter.
There were plenty of warriors to choose from,
all of whom would be perfectly willing to be
recognized as "principal," and who would feel
aggrieved were they overlooked in the selection.
There were a number of interpreters also.

I first selected an interpreter, Charles E.
Gueru, a Frenchman from France (a term used
on the river in contradistinction to a French-

man from Canada), who had long been associated with the Sioux, having first come among
them under the auspices of the old North-Western Fur Company. He was perfectly familiar
with their language and customs, and, having
married a Brulé Sioux woman, was looked
upon as belonging to that band. With his assistance I chose the warriors, somewhat with
reference to their known friendship for Spotted
Tail. Swift Bear was also a firm friend of the
latter.

I then sent word to the chiefs and warriors
concerned that I wanted to see them, and, upon
their arrival, informed them for the first time
of the order which I had received. I was somewhat astonished to hear that they did not care
to visit their Great Father in Washington, who,
as they understood, lived a great way off, much
farther than they cared to go; if he wanted to
see them, he might at least come half way.
They remained steadfast in this decision, and
finally departed without giving their consent to
make the visit. Spotted Tail, however, went
back to his camp with the understanding that
he should return in a few days.

The subject was allowed to rest, although it
was soon noised abroad that the Great Father
desired to see some of the principal chiefs and
warriors, and I had to listen to several applications, made by ambitious braves, who thought

that they were as good representatives as the ones already invited who did not desire to go. Fortunately, there was but one answer to make, which lessened complications, and this was that the President had sent for the ones whom he wished to see, and that I could not take any one else until he should order me to do so.

At the end of three days Spotted Tail was again at the agency, and I had an interview with him by himself upon the subject of the visit; but he was still disinclined to accept the invitation. His principal reason for refusing was, that he would probably see a great many things which would be new and strange to him, and upon his return his friends would come to his lodge and ask him to tell what he had seen, and that, while he might give a true account, his hearers, after they had listened a while, would leave his lodge, one by one, and say to his friends, "Spotted Tail tells lies since he has been to the Great Father's country, and the white men that he has seen have made bad medicine for him," and that in the end there would be none coming to his lodge, and he would be left alone—meaning that he would lose his chieftainship.

I reminded him that he had often told me of his desire to help his people, but now, when he had the opportunity to do so, he seemed disinclined to make good his assertions, and that he

could go and see the Great Father and many
things new and strange to him, but that he
need not talk about them on his return, but
merely tell his friends what the Great Father
had said, and that any promises the Great
Father might make I was sure would be ful-
filled.

He was inclined to be persuaded, but wanted
an interview with Swift Bear before fully deciding. The next day he called, and informed
me that he and Swift Bear had decided to go.
There was no trouble about the warriors; they
would follow the chiefs.

Before the time appointed for our departure
Spotted Tail brought in Two Strike from his
village, and expressed his desire that the latter
should accompany the party, while Swift Bear
brought his friend and neighbor, Fire Thunder,
with a similar request.

While I had no doubt but that this addition
to the party would be advantageous, I could
not comply for the reasons before stated; but
softened my refusal by representing to the ap-
plicants the necessity of some chiefs remaining
at home who would have sufficient authority
to govern, not only their people, but those left
without a chief by the absence of Spotted Tail
and Swift Bear.

The warriors selected were Fast Bear, a Brulé,
and Yellow Hair, an Ogallala. The former

was known as an influential warrior in Spotted
Tail's camp, while Yellow Hair had made himself conspicuous, a short time before, by an encounter in Fire Thunder's camp, in which he
had killed his assailant, and had thus still further established his reputation among the Indians as a great warrior.

CHAPTER XXII.

CHIEFS CONSENT TO GO—PREPARATIONS—EN ROUTE TO
YANKTON.

THE consent of the chiefs having been gained, the other arrangements were soon made. The Indians were offered clothing similar to that of white men, but preferred their own. The exposure of the copper-colored skin of the Sioux warrior does not seem out of place in his own home; but, now that he was to journey to another land, and among people whose ideas of dress differed entirely from his own, some additions must be made to his ordinary costume of blanket, leggins, breech cloth and moccasins, in order to make him presentable. So shirts were provided, and, as the Indians put them on as flowing robes, with no part tucked away, they made a considerable covering. They did not harmonize with the native costume, particularly while the wearers were still among their friends, but use soon familiarized the change. Some cover for the head was suggested, but that was too much of an innovation for the present.

Transportation by the river was uncertain, as it was early in the season and steamboats had not yet completed their long trips up the river so as to be returning. There was no stage, but one was improvised out of a rough lumber wagon.

On the 17th of May, the day appointed for our departure, the party presented themselves, each carrying a small sack made of dressed hide, and containing personal effects, but of what particular kind I was never able to discover. We were escorted to the bank of the river, which we were to cross, by a large concourse of Indians, mostly women, prominent among whom were the wives of the travelers. All the squaws chanted farewells in their usual piercing voices, which could be heard long after we had reached the further bank of the Missouri, and were on our way across the prairie.

Our first halting place was White Swan, directly opposite to Fort Randall, and about twenty-three miles from Whetstone Agency. White Swan could boast of an Indian trader's store and one authorized ranch, the latter being the headquarters of the stage company and the end of the route from Yankton.

A few tepees were scattered in the brush near by, belonging to the Yankton Sioux, whose reservation extended to this point, although their agency buildings were fifteen miles down the river. The Indian families located here were of the lowest kind—a demoralized set who hang around frontier garrisons.

Our host the ranchman furnished fair meals, but the beds could not be praised, except as offering a rich field of inquiry to an entomologist. This dismal halting place was gladly left behind at break of day. We had fifteen miles to ride before breakfast at Yankton Agency, and, if fresh morning air and about three hours of shaking up would give an appetite, we certainly should have one. The actual experiment proved, on arrival, that we did possess the real article, which was appeased at the agency ranch by food of the kind known as plain and substantial.

The Yankton Indians called upon Spotted Tail and others of our party, holding necessarily a short interview, as we had sixty miles more to make that day before reaching Yankton. The principal chief of the Yankton Sioux, Strike-the-Ree, had many things to say, and various messages to send by Spotted Tail to his Great Father. He also loaned a pipe to be used in the council at Washington. His interview was only terminated by our departure.

Our next stop was at Bon Homme, where we had the ranchman's square meal. Thence on to Yankton, arriving at the latter point late in the evening. Thus far the Indians had seen nothing particularly new; the same stretches of prairie, dotted here and there with buttes, and crossed by running streams on their course to the Missouri. They had never been over the road, but showed their knowledge of prairie craft by indicating, as far as the eye could reach, the location of streams and woodland and the general contour of the land, and having an almost intuitive knowledge of camping ground.

Yankton was the largest town ever seen by any of them except Spotted Tail, who had some years before been confined as a prisoner of war at Fort Leavenworth.

At Yankton they were for the first time surrounded by a plurality of white men, turning the tables on their life-long associations. Here were presented to their view the works of men, which, by their extent and grandeur as compared to their own, were to be a constant source of increasing wonder as they continued their journey eastward.

Although it was late in the evening when we arrived at Yankton, we were subjected to our first interview. The show had commenced. The official dignitaries must, of course, see the Indians, together with the sovereigns — the people generally. The Indians shook hands

and said "how," but gradually put on their
most approved stoical looks and undemonstrative manner. During the day they had been
talking and laughing and observing everything,
but now they went into their shells and staid
there, and were not to be drawn out by any remarks of the visitors, some of which were complimentary, some pitying, and some savage.

The last questions were asked and the last
suggestions made after midnight, when the
party were allowed to retire.

CHAPTER XXIII.

A SHORT association with white men had produced one visible effect upon the travelers, for on their appearance next morning they asked for an addition to their dress, in the shape of hats. These were procured, of the soft felt kind usually worn in the West, the stove pipe hat of the East not having penetrated to Yankton.

The party had still sixty-five miles to travel by stage before reaching Sioux City and the railroad. While the stage company was perfectly willing to accept our six fares, they would not guarantee seats, but proposed merely the same privileges that they offered to the general public, namely, to get a seat anywhere on the conveyance, inside or out, or to walk or run while holding on behind. The honored chiefs and warriors of an aboriginal State could not be subjected to such vicissitudes, while the guests of an enlightened nation; therefore private conveyances were obtained, and we were soon on our way to a land where stages were fast going out of fashion.

A short ride and we crossed the James River (commonly called "the Jim"), which courses north and south nearly the whole length of Dakota, and upon whose banks many camps have been made by those cousins of the Brulés and Ogallalas who live east of the Missouri; then we passed through the Indian-named towns, Vermillion and Elk Point, and finally, after a tiresome ride, crossed the Big Sioux River, into which, only four or five years before, many a Yankton Sioux had ridden his pony to drink, while hunting buffalo a short distance above, and had camped upon its banks while his wives prepared his robes for use. Now the white man occupied the land, and the busy hum of industry had driven the buffalo to the more quiet prairies north and west.

The pipe stone quarries, where material for the red stone pipe is found in abundance, are near the banks of this stream, a hundred miles or so north from where we crossed. This pipe is extensively used by the Indians of the plains. It is said that the quarry was neutral to all the different tribes, but it is probably nearer the truth that the Indians of Minnesota and Eastern Dakota had a monopoly of the quarry, and bartered the pipes made from the red soft stone with those with whom they came in contact.

The Sioux have both traded and fought with their neighbors from time out of mind, being like white men in this respect.

Crossing the Big Sioux, we drive into Sioux City. Here we pass a night at the St. Elmo, with about the same experience as at Yankton, and next morning take passage on the cars drawn by the Indian's "fire horse." Spotted Tail and Swift Bear had, a few years before, been honored by short rides on the Union Pacific road at North Platte Station; but the warriors, Fast Bear and Yellow Hair, had never traveled faster than a pony's gallop. The last two looked about them with some curiosity, but the general observer would not have discovered any unusual excitement. The visiting party had, from the time of starting, a thorough appreciation of the dignity of deportment required by their position as representative men and Indians.

We had to make more southing from Sioux City, until, at Missouri Valley Junction, we struck at a right angle the Northwestern Railroad.

Here the Indians were introduced to that modern luxury of travel, a sleeping car, and had a state room to themselves, the privacy of which they thoroughly enjoyed, as in their

short ride from Sioux City they had been subjected to much annoyance from inquisitive passengers. Many of these being Western men,
and in their own opinion familiar with Indians,
tried to engage them in conversation, but always signally failed. An Indian's stolidity
would take the pith out of the most inveterate
questioner. Failing to obtain the least reply
from the Indians, they next turned upon the
interpreter, who, with the imperturbable good
nature of a Frenchman, repeated the same
story as many times as it could possibly be
told in the five hours' run to Missouri Valley
Junction.

The presence of the Indians aroused the ire
of the hardy frontiersman, as it did the curiosity of other passengers. He was, perhaps,
still stinging under losses at the hands of Indians, and gave his opinion of how they should
be treated; usually in the direction of the
speediest extermination. He would hang them,
shoot them, burn them, or anything else to
eliminate them, closing these gentle suggestions with a few oaths and a glare upon those
present, as much as to say he was looking for
the man who differed from him.

In the state room of the sleeping car the Indians escaped these annoyances, and passed the
time in their usual way—chatting, story telling,
and observing what was going on around them.

After eighteen hours on the Northwestern road, we arrived in Chicago, and were well cared for at the old Tremont, the prince of hotels before the great fire of 1871. Here the Indians, for the first time, came in contact with the results of metropolitan tastes, most of which are well represented in a modern hotel; spacious halls, reception and dining rooms, pier glasses which magnified in number the costly embellishments, and a table furnished to repletion with every dainty, were a surprise and comfort to a white man coming from the West after a long sojourn on the frontier. What would it be to Indians who had never even imagined anything of the kind? So far as any outward manifestation could be an indication, they produced no effect whatever. These savages entered the spacious dining hall for the first time, with the same composure that they would a council lodge. Walking single file, according to rank, they took their seats at the table with all the nonchalance of the best-bred white man in the land. I knew that the table furniture was entirely new to them, but their quick eye and keen observation enabled them to follow instantly the manners of those with whom they were associated. The use of the knife and of the silver fork were confounded a little at first; but then in Europe, the fountain of our table manners, it is an open

question which shall be used in conveying food
from the plate to the mouth. The Sioux etiquette requires only a knife, the fingers taking
the place of the fork. A good-sized piece, cut
from the roast or stew, is grasped at one end
by the fingers and seized by the teeth at the
other, while a sharp knife is brought down
upon the morsel, severing it at a proper distance from the mouth. This process is repeated
until the remainder is of the proper size for an
ordinary mouthful, and requires more dexterity
than the proper use of knife and fork.

The napkin was at first a mystery to the
travelers, but observation soon taught them to
use it instead of the back of the hand, as was
their custom at home. After a little experience
they ate slowly and rather sparingly of what
was set before them, and awaited the arrival of
the various courses with as much ease and
composure as any high-bred individual who
takes no note of time.

The table manners of the Indians were a great
disappointment to the general public.

Whenever they entered a dining hall they
attracted the gaze of all in the room, while the
extra waiters and female attachés of the hotel
crowded the side doors, and gazed and gazed,
much to the annoyance of the (in this respect)
better bred Indians. I often heard the excla-
mation, "Why, these Indians eat just like

white people!" Michael and Biddy, fresh
from the other side, expected them to feed like
wild animals.

CHAPTER XXIV.

SUMPTUOUS SURROUNDINGS—VIEWS OF THOSE REMOTE FROM
INDIANS—HOW DEALT WITH IN THE PAST—HOW THEY
SHOULD BE TREATED NOW—ARRIVAL IN WASHINGTON.

LEAVING Chicago we proceed on our journey in the same comfortable manner; the
Indians occupying a state room in the Pullman
car. They are fast becoming educated in their
tastes, but in any just appreciation of their
surroundings are children still. They have no
conception of the fact that each hour they are
traveling what would be to them an ordinary
day's journey on their ambling ponies. It
never enters their minds to make any compari-
son between their present luxurious surroundings of polished wood, rich tapestries and
gilded cornices and the rude interior of their
smoky tepees.

To them the horse is still the perfection
of means of locomotion, and the tepee unsurpassed as a haven of rest and comfort. What
care they for railroads and gorgeous uphol-
stery. These contrivances of white men, so

wonderful in their perfection, arouse no more
than a slight curiosity. Their origin and the
means applied to bring them to perfection are
no more to these savages, than the origin of
the eternal hills, or the running streams of the
prairie.

We are now passing through States whose
inhabitants have long since forgotten the savage war whoop and bloody trail familiar to
their ancestors. By the policy of that day
and the treaties of that time, the Indians had
been removed from occupation of this land to
the unknown West, there, in time, to harass
by their presence another generation of fron-
tiers men, who, in their turn, strive to drive the
red men still farther west from what has now
become a neighboring State. The original
inhabitants of these States, so far as they were
concerned, solved the ever-recurring Indian
question by having the Indian removed from
their own immediate neighborhood, and their
descendants eventually forgot his existence,
save in history and legendry.

So, now, our visiting party are interviewed
by a more kindly-disposed people, who begin
to talk entirely of the wrongs done to the
Indian, how he has been cheated by the Government and his agent, and robbed and killed
by the pioneer, and more than intimate that he
would make a good friend and neighbor, if he

had not been cheated and driven away from his home, and could now live there in the moral atmosphere of the present. The past has always been entirely wrong in its treatment of the Indian. Agricultural implements and seeds and morality are all that are needed now to change the savage, held at bay somewhere in the west, to a peaceful and law-abiding citizen. A far-off view of the original occupant of the land enables them to see both sides of the question, and to realize that the Indian has been driven from boundary to boundary across each State until, now that he can go no farther, he has turned back again to shame past generations, who were governed too much by interest and not enough by the philanthropic views of the present inhabitants of the land. Another indication of the distance we have traveled is shown in the rural interviewer, who wants to know if these Indians are real " Si-oxes," a mistake in pronunciation which would not have occurred farther west. We find, too, an increasing desire to see real wild Indians from the plains, who have not lost the art of killing and scalping. Did they know that the Indians each carry a good-sized revolver and sharp scalping knife in their belts, they would be still more anxious to see them.

We finally reach Pittsburgh, where we make a short halt, and meet Hon. Felix Bruno, a

philanthropist, and member of the Peace Commission, who is making an earnest effort to
ameliorate the present condition of the Indians
in the far west. Spotted Tail and the others
do not take much interest in Mr. Bruno's expressed desire to improve their present state of
affairs. The former has heard from a great
many others that he is never to be cheated any
more.

At Harrisburg we make our easting, and
change our course to the south for Baltimore
and Washington, and arrive at our jouney's
end after one week of travel. The Indians are
fifteen hundred miles from their homes, in a
city where they are to be impressed with the
dignity and power of the country of their
Great Father, whom they have come so far to
interview. An unpretentious hotel, connected
with the Washington House, is designated as
the resting place for the delegation, who now
learn, for the first time, that they are to be
joined by some of their brothers and neighbors
under the famous chief Red Cloud.

CHAPTER XXV.

VISITORS AT THEIR HOTEL—INVITATIONS TO FAIRS AND EXHI-
BITIONS—THEIR ISRAELITISH DESCENT—CHEROKEES AND
WHITE BLOOD.

SPOTTED TAIL and his friends were somewhat worn with the fatigues of the long
journey, and were given a day of rest in their
hotel before they paid any official visits. But
they were not allowed much real rest or quiet,
and received many calls. Some of their visitors
had been among Indians upon the plains, and
felt an interest in all red men; others had a
slight knowledge of the Sioux language, and
wanted to bring it to a test by an interview;
others desired to make inquiry about a chief
or warrior whom they had known. Invitations
of every kind were received, by which the delegation were urged to visit some exhibition, art
gallery or photographic establishment. These
invitations were usually delivered in person,
and if they were declined the party tendering
them seemed to consider it equivalent to an implied intention, on the part of those having

the Indians in charge, to favor some unknown
rival. There were invitations to church festi-
vals and charitable fairs, offering inducements
to the Indians in the way of strawberries and
fine floral displays. One such invitation spoke
of the display of flags of all nations which
would be made, and which, the writer said,
would probably be very interesting to the
Indians, reminding them also, that the benevolent association to be assisted, was worthy the
support of all good men.

When Spotted Tail was asked if he desired
to attend these festivities he invariably declined.

After a day or so of waiting this chief
became impatient, and complained that he had
not come to Washington to be made a show of,
but to see the Great Father, which he wanted
to do and then go home to his people. Apparently he was not interested in sight seeing, or
fond of being the center of the public gaze.

The party refused to visit a photographer
and be photographed. Spotted Tail, with all
his intelligence, was Indian enough to say that
he considered it bad medicine to sit for a picture, meaning that it would bring him bad
luck ; and whatever he said was followed by
the others. A gentleman from the Smith
sonian Institute labored long and faithfully to
obtain a plaster of Paris model of Spotted

Tail's head.   The interpreter endeavored to obtain his consent to submit to the preliminaries, and offered himself to be experimented upon to show the process.   The Indians watched with the greatest interest while the interpreter lay prostrate with quills stuck in his nostrils and the coating of plaster upon his face.   They considered the operation great fun, but decided that it was bad medicine, and no amount of persuasion could change their minds.

A reverend gentleman called to pay his respects, and being admitted to the room in which the Indians were seated, passed from one to another making some remark to each ; commenting on their journey hither, hoping that they were enjoying themselves and trusting that they would find their visit pleasant and profitable in every way.   He then took a position in the center of the room, and commenced a lecture, opening by remarking that it afforded him great pleasure to see them and talk with them, as he had long held the theory that they were descendants of the ancient Israelites ; that many of their present customs were similar to those of the latter, and he was just going on to explain the route which the Israelites must have taken to reach this continent, when I interrupted the lecturer to inform him that the Indians did not understand the English language, and that any remarks he had to make would have to be interpreted. This was quite a surprise to the gentleman, but he was introduced to the interpreter, through whom he continued his discourse, and the latter had to translate many strange words into the Sioux language. The chiefs and warriors made no reply whatever. To all appearance they would have been as much interested in the demonstration of a problem from Euclid, as in the question of their Jewish descent. Spotted Tail was searching for more supplies and a new agency and not after the origin of his ancient progenitors, whoever they might be.

There was no end to their visitors. A delegation of Cherokees from the Indian Territory called and had to enter into a description of themselves through the interpreter, to convince the Dakota delegation that they were real Indians. The blood of the Cherokees had been mingled with that of white men until but little of the former was left; but they still talked of unfulfilled treaties with the white men's Government, so there was this bond of common interest between them and the Sioux.

CHAPTER XXVI.

FIRST INTERVIEW WITH THE COMMISSIONER — VISITS AT
GENERAL SHERMAN'S, SMITHSONIAN INSTITUTE AND MOUNT
VERNON.

SOON after their arrival the delegation were
invited to call on the Commissioner of Indian Affairs. The ceremonies were short. After
handshaking all around, the Indians seated
themselves and filled the pipe of peace, such
as desired taking a few whiffs as it passed
around. Spotted Tail never used tobacco on
any occasion, either here or at his home.

The Commissioner expressed himself as being
glad to see his visitors, commended the peaceful relations existing between them and the
Government, and said that the President had
sent for them, to see himself what they wanted
in order to continue the good will, and would
hold an interview with them and friends as
soon as Red Cloud arrived.

Spotted Tail, as usual, was the spokesman.
He did not express any particular amount of
happiness over the interview, but said that

when he was more rested from his journey he would make known his wants. He accepted, with some show of pleasure, an invitation for the party to visit General Sherman at his residence, for both he and Swift Bear had met the General on the plains. At evening the party were driven in carriages to the General's house, where they were cordially entertained. They were much interested in looking over his collection of Indian curiosities from all parts of the country, and of weapons and trinkets from Japan and from the barbarous peoples of the South Sea Islands. Mrs. Sherman and her daughters showed every attention to their blanketed guests, and feasted them upon strawberries, ice cream and cake—articles too ethereal to be much sought after by the Indians, but apparently enjoyed by them on this occasion.

Instructions had been given me to allow the Indians every opportunity to see all objects of interest which they might desire to. As far as could be ascertained, they did not desire to see anything, and so I selected such places as I thought might amuse and instruct them.

The Smithsonian Institute afforded them a day of entertainment in looking over the stuffed birds and animals, and the various arms and utensils collected from different parts of the world. Any animal or bird with which they were familiar reminded them of their prairie home, and caused many animated discussions. Catlin's collection of portraits of Western Indians made a study for them. They readily singled out the members of different tribes, many of whom it would have afforded them great pleasure to kill and scalp, could they have been found lurking about the Institute in flesh and blood.

They visited the theater for the first time, and amid brilliant lights and the bright colors of the decorator's art, and in the presence of the audience, were calm and stoical as usual. The stormy passion of the hero in the play, and the stealthy tread of the heavily whiskered, rouged and armed villain, interested them; and the subsequent encounter between the two, with swords clashing together with such force as to bring sparks of fire from their blades, fixed their attention; or when fire-arms were the weapons in the deadly contest, and discharged at such an elevation above the victim as would lead them to suppose that his vulnerable parts were hidden away somewhere in the flies, they were amused and astonished to see the victim fall dead at the discharge; but they were not wrought up to any degree of emotion. Their medicine men could handle a long knife or a gun more dexterously to deceive, and the whole scenic effect fell far below the wild pantomime of the war dance.

They were taken a pleasant sail down the Potomac as far as Mount Vernon, where they passed part of a day in viewing the grounds and lounging under the shade of the trees, enjoying an undisturbed siesta. They saw the tomb of the first Great Father, but did not, as was said at the time, reach through the grating of the iron door to shake hands with him and say "How."

They passed through the old mansion and looked at its mementoes, and while so doing were decoyed into a reception room, where the good woman in charge of the Mount Vernon estate took them in hand, after a fashion similar to their reverend friend interested in their remote ancestors, the Israelites. She commenced telling Spotted Tail and Swift Bear what the women of the country were trying to do in the way of purchasing the ground where rested the mortal remains of the father of his country, and was so much interested in her subject that it was with difficulty she could be stopped, and informed, as usual in such cases, that the Indians could not understand her remarks unless they were interpreted into the Sioux language. As the Indians were rather pleased with the lady's attentions, and were seemingly interested, she was inclined to continue her remarks in spite of remonstrances to the contrary; but finally the interpreter interposed, and gave the

Indians an idea of the great work which the women had in hand, and of the desire of this lady that they should become interested in the scheme and contribute, but the remarks did not have the desired effect. The chieftains did not order drafts upon their royal exchequers, nor drop coin from their hands, for the reason that they did not possess one or the other. Had they been importuned at their homes, they might have contributed ponies, buffalo robes, or bows and arrows, their principal articles of wealth and mediums of exchange, for they are far from miserly with their possessions. It is doubtful, however, if they could ever have been greatly interested in the scheme to purchase Mount Vernon.

We returned to the city and visited the Botanical Garden and the Patent Office buildings. The former place, with its bright flowers and rich scent of roses, was looked over unnoticed, their æsthetic tastes being entirely uncultivated. At the latter place the great collection of all conceivable articles that in any way enter into the economy of civilization failed to interest the guests of the nation.

They began to manifest a dislike to the restraints of civilization, and were impatient to come to an understanding with the Government and return to their native prairies.

CHAPTER XXVII.

MEETING OF SPOTTED TAIL AND RED CLOUD——CALL AT THE
WHITE HOUSE.

THE renowned Red Cloud, Chief of the Ogallala Sioux, with a number of his warriors
and their wives, had arrived. There had been
an intimation that this Chief would manifest
resentment towards Spotted Tail when they
should meet, for the part the latter had taken
in the affray with the late Big Mouth, but there
was no demonstration of feeling. The Chief of
the Ogallalas greeted the Chief of the Brulés with
all the seeming cordiality that is usually shown
when friendly Indians meet. They advanced
towards each other, shook hands with some
show of warmth, and each said " How," when
the greeting was over, and they subsided into
pleasant chit-chat, as though no long separa-
tion had taken place. It was understood by
Red Cloud that Spotted Tail had sufficiently
condoned for his act in killing one of the house
of Red Cloud, by making prompt payment of a
stipulated number of ponies to Blue Horse, the

next of kin, and whatever resentment might exist was silenced by the fact that aboriginal law had been vindicated.

General Smith had brought Red Cloud and his party from Fort Fetterman. They were provided for at the same hotel with Spotted Tail, so they mingled together freely and discussed their common interests, their complaints, which were uppermost in their minds. After the arrival of Red Cloud, Spotted Tail and his friends were accorded an interview with the President, the design being made apparent that the latter Chief should be recognized first and given the place of honor.

When Spotted Tail and Swift Bear and their warriors were informed that the President desired to see them, they exhibited more interest than they had at any other occurrence. They were solicitous about their personal appearance, and examined themselves critically in their little hand mirrors, which the Indians carry at all times as an indispensable article. The Chiefs had passed beyond the age of using paint to any great extent, in making their toilets, although where the hair was parted a dash of red was applied. Any stray whiskers, that had grown to sufficient length to be seized, were pulled out with small steel tweezers, which they have for this purpose. Their hair was arranged as usual, with a small braided scalp lock gathered up from the crown of the head, to which an eagle feather is attached, while a side lock, bound with strips of otter skin, is trained to hang forward on the shoulder. This was all readjusted, and the toilets of the two Chiefs were completed. The warriors made similar preparations, but added a modest allowance of color to their faces.

The party arrived at the White House in carriages, and were immediately granted a private audience by the President. The Secretary of War and the Secretary of the Treasury were present at first, but did not remain long. After the usual handshaking, the Indians were shown seats, and the President talked to them in a plain, direct way, that engrossed their attention from the commencement. He assured them of his intention to do all in his power to provide for them under their treaty, and explained to them that he was dependent upon Congress to furnish the money to be expended for them, but hoped that sufficient would be given to meet their wants. He reminded them of what was expected on their part, that they must remain at peace, and if they themselves could not learn to cultivate the soil and become self supporting, that they must bring up their children to do so.

The Indians signified their assent to this talk from their Great Father with many

"Hows." President Grant's manner of expressing himself produced a lasting impression upon them, and they undoubtedly remember the interview to this day.

Both Spotted Tail and Swift Bear were a little embarrassed, the only time I ever saw them so in the least degree. The latter commenced to fill the pipe furnished by Strike-the-Ree for this occasion, but Spotted Tail said something to him which made him stop, and it was not used. Spotted Tail, being called upon, made a very fair statement of his case. He was in the presence of the Great Father, where he had never been before, and as he undoubtedly had the interest of his people at heart, he was fully imbued with the importance of his task, and very desirous to make the best of his opportunity ; so lost much of his usual self-contained manner.

He reminded the President of some of the provisions of the treaty made with them, and among other things, desired to have his agency at some other point than Whetstone. He wanted it away from the Missouri River, where he said there was too much whiskey. By going back from the river, he would be where bad white men could not trade with his people, and demoralize them with intoxicating drink. He made no allusion to himself, but talked of his people and their wants, and was a most

faithful advocate. The President promised
Spotted Tail that he should have an agency
anywhere he wanted it, within the Sioux reservation.

The ladies of the White House were present,
and were interested spectators. The President
gave Spotted Tail a handsome meerschaum
pipe, with his monogram carved upon it, while
the ladies presented tobacco and a silver match
box. The Indians were very much pleased with
the interview and its results.

From the White House they went to the
Treasury building, and were conducted through
its various departments. They were shown vast
sums of money stowed away in vaults, and
taken in an elevator to the top of the building
to see the process of printing bank bills, and
the working of the hydraulic press of many
tons power. Thence through General Spin-
ner's Department, where they watched with interest the fair women counting and sorting
various denominations of bank bills and frac-
tional currency.

After their return to the hotel the party were
quite talkative, and dilated upon the experiences of the day. Spotted Tail was very much
impressed with his interview with President
Grant, but he and Swift Bear could not understand how the President was waiting to receive
money from Congress, as he had said, when

they had just seen a large building full of it, which belonged to him.

The financial problem was explained to them by the interpreter, but they still expressed their inability to comprehend it. Their day's visit had suggested another thought. Spotted Tail wanted to know, for the benefit of himself and party, how it was that the President had but one wife, as he had been informed, when they had seen so many handsome women to choose from in the Treasury. The interpreter had to again come to the rescue and explain that the white man's laws allowed only one wife at a time, and that even if he were President, he could not increase the number.

The Chiefs and warriors thought their customs in this respect were better.

The day had been satisfactory in its results, and now that their object was accomplished, the Indians wanted to know when they could go back to their homes.

CHAPTER XXVIII.

THE addition of the Red Cloud party increased the number of Indians by twenty, so that the upper part of the old Beverly House was well filled with nomads. The walk in front of the hotel was thronged with spectators who wished to see wild Indians, and it often required the assistance of the police to clear a passage to the carriages, when they went out for an official visit or on a sight-seeing expedition.

The two delegations were invited to call upon the Commissioner, where they would see the Secretary of the Interior. The increase in the number of Indians, and the growing interest in them, augmented the spectators wherever they went, and on this occasion the delegations had much difficulty in passing through the packed hallways of the Interior building, the chiefs being somewhat ruffled by the jostling of the crowd.

After entering the room the Indians were seated, and the Commissioner introduced the Secretary. The Secretary addressed the circle of Indians as follows :

"When we heard that the Chiefs of the Sioux nation wanted to come to Washington to see the President, and the officers of the Government, we were glad. We were glad that they themselves said they wanted to come. We know that when people are so far apart as we are from the Sioux, it is very hard to see each other and to know what each one wants. But when we see each other face to face, we can understand better what is really right, and what we ought to do. The President and myself, and all the officers of the Government, want to do the thing that is right. While you are here, therefore, we shall want you to tell us what is in your own hearts, all you feel, and what your condition is, so that we may have a perfect understanding, that we may make a peace that shall last forever. In coming here you have seen that this is a very great people, and we are growing all the time. We want to find out the condition of things in the Sioux country, so that we may make satisfactory treaties. In a day or two the President himself will see the chiefs, and, in the meantime, we want them to prepare to tell him what they have to say, and we will make our answer,

honestly as we mean. We want also to use
our influence so that there shall not only be
peace between the Indians and whites, but so
that there shall be no more trouble about difficulties between different bands of Indians."

The Secretary then addressed a few words to
Spotted Tail, thanking him for being present
at the interview, and telling him that he was
glad of the good will he had for the whites.

This was supposed to be the end of the interview, but Red Cloud had something to say,
and spoke in his usual arrogant style, as follows :

" My friends, I have come a long way to see
you and the Great Father, but somehow, after I
have reached here, you do not look at me.
When I heard the words of the Great Father per-
mitting me to come, I came right away, and left
my women and children. I want you to give
them rations and a load of ammunition to kill
game with. I wish you would telegraph to my
people about it. Tell them I arrived all right."

The Secretary promised to telegraph Red
Cloud's people that he had arrived safely, and
that his other requests would receive careful
attention.

Red Cloud felt the slight in not having been
invited to see the President when Spotted Tail
had his interview, and this is what he meant
when he said that his friends did not seem to

see him, now that he had arrived.   This chief
is a typical representative of his race, who are
often egotistical, arrogant, and abounding in
self-esteem.

After leaving the Interior Building, such of
the party as desired to do so visited the Capitol, the House being in session and considering
the Indian appropriation bill.   They filed into
the gallery, and taking front seats, looked
down upon the President's Council, as they
called it, attracting much attention from the
members, who could see the chieftains complacently fanning themselves, while the former
voted their supplies.

The party were taken to the dome of the
capitol, where they could have an extended
view of the city and adjacent country, and
within of the rotunda.   They realized that
they were a long distance from the ground,
and soon desired to retrace their steps, and be
upon solid earth once more.   The reception
room of the President, furnished in marble,
was looked at, and the bronze and gilt of
the chandeliers were to them the most attractive features here.   Some marble busts of
Indians attracted their attention on account
of the subject.

They utterly failed to realize the accumulated
amount of toil and treasure represented in this
vast building.   Their uncultivated minds passed

it by without study or thought.   Nevertheless,
these same savages were the leaders of a people,
who, stirred by the magic of their rude eloquence and personal prowess, could put a fighting force into the field, the recountal of whose
horrid deeds would stir the nation, and to suppress which would cost in treasure far more
than this magnificent building.   So, why should
they not be conciliated ?

CHAPTER XXIX.

VISIT THE ARSENAL AND NAVY YARD UNDER DIRECTION OF
THE SECRETARY OF WAR AND NAVY.

WORD was sent to me that the Indians were
to be shown through the Arsenal and
Navy Yard, the object being to impress them
with the power and greatness of the Government, and its many appliances for destroying
its enemies.

Under the direction of the Secretary of the
Interior and the Commissioner of Indian Affairs, the two delegations were first taken to
the Arsenal, and shown through the grounds
by the Secretary of War. In everything per-
taining to warfare the Indians took a lively interest, and examined minutely all implements
that came under their keen observation. A
twenty-inch Columbiad, mounted on its immense iron carriage, was in position on the
banks of the Potomac, and was manœuvred by
a squad of artillery men for the delectation of
the Indian guests. The mammoth powder used
in loading this huge cannon was shown to the

red men, and elicited some astonishment on account of the size of its grains, almost as large as nut coal, and very different from the coveted fine-grained rifle powder in use among them. They were still more surprised when they saw a hundred pound sack of this coarse powder used for a single charge, and the thousand pound solid shot hoisted to the cannon's mouth by means of machinery, and then allowed to roll to the bottom of the bore.

The machinery for loading did not work smoothly, and much time was consumed before the cannon was ready for discharge.

The Indians watched the operation, and commented upon the length of time it took for loading. They united in condemning the huge destroyer as being of no practical use. As they expressed it, they could ride all around such a big gun and over the hills and far away before it could be loaded and discharged; besides, it was so heavy it could not be moved, and they did not see why any one should want to come near the monster and wait to be killed. Their own mode of warfare is perfection to them, and sea-coast defense has not been one of their studies.

They were promised by the interpreter a loud noise when the piece should be discharged—one that would startle them—but here again they were disappointed. The mammoth powder burnt slowly, and did not produce a sharp, ringing shock in the air, but a deep diapason not unpleasant to the ear, which reverberated along the shores of the Potomac, and was probably heard twenty miles away, but was lost upon the Indians. Had the concussion knocked them off their feet, its power would have impressed them.

The shot struck the water some three miles down the river, and threw up jets of water as it *ricocheted* over the surface, ending in a final splash and plunge.

Next a light field battery of four guns was rapidly loaded and fired at a target in the river, and, as the solid shot and shell and canister threw up the water near the target, the savage visitors were highly delighted, and acknowledged that it would make matters very lively for them to come in contact with such a battery on the prairie.

The Museum was visited, where the various arms in use, past and present, were exhibited; also the arms of foreign nations. Some models, dressed to show the different uniforms of soldiers in this and other countries, entertained them for a while.

From the Arsenal they were escorted to the Navy Yard, to be royally entertained by the Secretary of the Navy. The marines were in full dress, and so also were the officers of the navy stationed there. The marines were paraded in line, and presented arms to the princely visitors, while their band discoursed music. All the machinery in the yard was in operation, showing, among other things, the different processes in the manufacture of howitzers, and the various kinds of fixed ammunition for small arms—the leaden bullet, copper shell, percussion and powder. The huge trip hammer was set in motion, and used in forging an immense sheet anchor. Its mighty weight came down with such force as to shake the ground, and sent out huge scintillating sparks on all sides; but the Indians looked on with stoical indifference. They could not comprehend the wonderful mechanical contrivances exhibited before them.

After they had examined the various shops, they returned through one where howitzers were being turned down on a lathe, a sharp steel point cutting a thin, narrow strip of brass, which coiled up and dropped down as waste material. These bright ringlets attracted the notice of Spotted Tail and Red Cloud, and they asked permission to take some of them Of course this was granted, and all the Indians helped themselves, stowing away the bits of metal in the hidden mysteries of their blankets, as much pleased as any children. They had seen nothing else in the whole Navy Yard that aroused so much admiration as these bright strips of brass.

An iron-turreted monitor was lying at the wharf, with steam on hand sufficient to turn her turret, and the Indians were invited to inspect her. When told that the vessel was made entirely of iron, they doubted the statement, saying it was impossible for iron to float in water, and remained incredulous until it was suggested to them that they could try and cut the deck, which was within reach of the wharf, with their knives. Both Spotted Tail and Red Cloud tried the experiment, and having found, much to their astonishment, that the vessel was really all iron, they doubted the advisability of going on board, as there was danger of her sinking. They held quite a long consultation among each other on the subject, but finally decided to do so provided I would take the lead.

The chiefs followed very close upon my heels while on board, particularly when going below decks. The vessel was down in the water within a couple of feet of the upper deck, and, as they had noticed this, they concluded, when going down the steps of the companion way, that they must be under water, and insisted upon retracing their steps to the upper deck. None of the Indians wanted to stay long on board, and all were glad to step on shore when the inspection was over.

After they had gone through the yard, the
party were invited to the commanding officer's
quarters to partake of a collation which he
had ready for his guests, who, during their
whole visit, had been as well entertained as
any foreign prince or potentate could have
been.

CHAPTER XXX.

LEVEE AT PRESIDENTIAL MANSION GIVEN TO INDIANS.

ON the morning of June 6th, Spotted Tail and Red Cloud were notified that the President would see them and their respective followers at the White House that evening at seven o'clock. This was to be the great event to the Indians during their visit to Washington, and they spent most of the afternoon in arranging their toilets. Spotted Tail and friends having already seen the Great Father, did not fail to show their greater importance in consequence, and gave the Red Cloud party the benefit of their superior knowledge, by informing them of some points of etiquette which they thought might be useful to the latter.

Spotted Tail and party did not make any great change in their usual dress, contenting themselves with putting on clean white shirts, rearranging their hair with its simple eagle's feather, and applying a modest quantity of paint. They scrutinized themselves carefully in their hand mirrors, using the tweezer when necessary, and were ready for the entertainment.

But the Ogallalas shook out their eagle feather head dresses, and adjusted them to see if they were all right for the occasion. These grotesque head dresses, or war bonnets, are made of eagles' feathers, usually sewed into red flannel, and have a train extending from the head to the ground. With rude surroundings they are not only odd, but picturesque; but under the glare of gaslight and in sumptuous drawing rooms, they were rather too primitive to be admired. There were three or four of these fantastic head dresses in the Red Cloud party, and the latter daubed themselves more plentifully with paint than the Brulés had done. All the Indians wore their usual dark-blue blankets embroidered with beads, and leggins and moccasins similarly adorned. The four squaws were thickly painted on their faces, and were attired in plain short calico dresses, leggins, moccasins and blue blankets without embroidery or other ornamentation. They thus followed the usual law of nature, the male appearing in the more gorgeous plumage.

The delegation were driven to the White House in open barouches, and upon arrival were shown immediately into the East Room, which was decorated with flowers and brilliantly illuminated. The owners of the war bonnets, which were too cumbersome to be worn in a carriage, now carefully adjusted them, and all had a short time to view the room with its Turkish carpets, rich curtains and massive chandeliers, whose pendent prisms reflected a hundred lights. Soon the folding doors from the hall were thrown open, and the President entered, accompanied by his wife and daughter, the Cabinet Ministers and their wives, the Diplomatic Corps and their wives, and a few Senators and Representatives.

The Indians were seated on chairs and sofas, taking up nearly the whole south-east side of the large drawing-room. The Presidential party took position opposite to them, and upon an intimation from the Commissioner the interpreter introduced the Indians to the President and others, commencing with Spotted Tail. As they filed past each shook hands and gave the usual salutation "how!" first to the President and then to the other guests. This ceremony over the Indians retired to their side of the room, and the President, leading the way with a lady on his arm, addressed, through the interpreter, each of his Indian guests, while his white guests followed suite. Soon all were mingled together, some of the whites and Indians trying to hold conversation without an interpreter, but with poor success.

The chiefs, warriors and squaws were objects
of the liveliest interest, especially to the foreign
ministers and their wives, who evidently enjoyed the novel scene. The grotesque dress
and rude ornaments and trinkets worn by the
Indians were minutely examined, while the
squaws in their turn showed the usual interest
of their sex by admiring the dresses of the
white women present. They were especially
attracted by Madame G——, an Italian beauty,
who wore a dress beautifully ornamented with
Roman pearls. This lady noticing their admiration, tore off the rich pearl fringe and
gave some to each of them. They were highly
pleased, and immediately deposited the ornaments within the folds of their blankets.

The contrast between the white women and
the Indian women was extreme. The former
lithe and graceful, delicately formed, with
finely cut features, the peers and companions
of man; the latter heavy and awkward, coarse
featured and overworked, the menials and
slaves of their male companions. The elevation
of women by civilization and enlightenment,
and her low estate under the rule of savages
were here boldly outlined.

After an hour or so of mutual examination, the doors were thrown open into the
broad hall, and the green, blue and red rooms,
and thence into the State dining-room, where

another surprise met the gaze of the savages.
The State dining table was handsomely decorated and mirrored by a glass partially hidden
by its rich gold and silver ornaments, dishes,
glasses, flowers and bouquets, and covered with
fruits, ices, creams and confections.   It was a
tempting feast to the eye of the civilized
guests, but in strange contrast to any that the
mind of the savage could conceive.   Nevertheless, when ranged about the table and helped
from its bountiful dishes, the Indians were far
from reluctant in partaking of luxuries which
they had never tasted before.   They were
shown every attention by their white friends.
The President's wife and daughter, and the
wives of the foreign ministers were assiduous
in helping Spotted Tail, Red Cloud and the
warriors to the good things from the table ;
while the President himself and other high
functionaries waited upon the squaws.   The
Indians showed good taste in drinking sparingly of the wine offered them.   Their deportment
in this respect corresponded with their usual
dignified and courtly bearing when in the
presence of strangers.   The repast over, the
guests repaired again to the east room, and
mingled freely together for a time.   Miss
Nellie Grant and a young lady friend presented each one with a bouquet.   The Indians
hardly knew what to do with them, but man-

aged to keep them in their hands in imitation
of the other guests. President Grant inquired
of Spotted Tail the number of his children,
and was answered eleven He then said that
he would take one of the boys and have him
educated and taken care of by the Government.

Spotted Tail said he would think about it.
The only son old enough at this time to leave
the parental tepee had, although only sixteen
years of age, gained lasting glory among his
people by killing and scalping a Pawnee, and
was on the high road to a chieftainship—a distinction more prized by his father than the
tame life offered by the President in the paths
of education.

I subsequently reminded Spotted Tail several
times of this offer, but he was never inclined to
move in the matter.

As the time for the Indians to take their
leave drew near, they expressed themselves as
well pleased with the evening, and, after again
shaking hands all around, were driven back to
the hotel. Thus ended what was to the guests
of both races an unusual reception, and one
not likely to again occur at the White House.
After their return to the hotel, the Indians
talked the affair over among themselves, and
Spotted Tail said that the white men had many
more good things to eat and drink than they

ever sent out to the Indians.   He was told that
that was because the white man had quitted
the war path and gone to farming.   The chief
exclaimed that he would do the same provided
he could be as well treated and live in as big a
house.

CHAPTER XXXI.

LEAVE WASHINGTON—STOP AT PHILADELPHIA—UNION LEAGUE
—U. S. MINT.

SPOTTED TAIL and his party having seen most of the notable objects in and about Washington, and having had a number of interviews with the President, the Secretary of the Interior, and the Commissioner of Indian Affairs, stated that the object of their visit was accomplished, and that they now desired to be on their way home. So a final interview was held with the Secretary and the Commissioner, and the former asked Spotted Tail if he had anything further to say before leaving. The Chief replied that he only wished to ask again that his young men might have Government protection in their annual buffalo hunt; that they must either hunt or starve, and in order to avoid collisions with other tribes, or with the whites, he wished some Government agent to go with them and keep them from fighting.

The Secretary told him that he should teach

his young men farming and other ways of
living, so that when there were no buffalos
they could have something else to eat. Very
good advice, but Spotted Tail was not inclined
to indorse the sentiment. In the course of the
talk the Secretary told him that he must expect
some trouble in his life ; that white men had
trouble; whereupon the Chief laughingly exclaimed :

" If you had had as much trouble in your life
as I have had in mine, you would have cut your
throat long ago. The Chief must have a stout
heart."

He also said that the last chiefs who had
visited the Great Father, had returned home
barefooted, and that their people had all
laughed at them. At this the Secretary said
that they should go home on horseback, and
the interview concluded to the satisfaction of
the Indians.

The party returned to the hotel to make preparations for their departure, and to say good-
bye to their friends, the Ogallalas, from whom
they were now to separate. My instructions
were to take them home by way of Philadelphia and New York, and to such other points
as would impress them with the extent of the
country and the number of its people. The
visiting party arrived in Philadelphia late in
the evening, and drove to the Continental,

where they were greeted by a large concourse
of people, who crowded the hallways and cor-
ridors of the hotel so that it was with the
utmost difficulty that an entrance was effected.

The spectators were so eager to see the
Indians, that it was only after much crowding
and jostling, that they were finally secured in
their rooms free from molestation for the night.

The next morning they were visited by a large
number of interested people who went through
the usual handshaking with the Indians, but
the latter gave no special welcome to any but
Mr. William Welsh.   This gentleman, form-
erly President of the Peace Commission, had
resigned that position to take independent
charge of the Sioux on the Missouri River, and
was doing most excellent work for them.

At about ten o'clock the delegation under
conduct of Mr. Welsh were driven to the
United States Mint.   A large crowd had assembled outside and stared eagerly at the Indians
as they passed into the office of the director,
who made a short speech of welcome, and presented to each of the Indians a silver medal
bearing the profile portraits of Washington
and Grant, with which they were much pleased.
They were then conducted through the various
departments, the operations of which were
briefly explained to them.   Having become
somewhat accustomed to sight-seeing, they ap-

parently took an interest in the explanations of the operation of coining money from bars of bullion. They were allowed to lift a box containing several thousand dollars in gold. In the assaying room the Governor showed them the process of separating silver from water, which especially attracted their attention. Spotted Tail remarked :

"You show us how to do it, but you don't teach us." Spotted Tail was like Polonius, still harping on his daughter, and wondered why it was, when the Great Father had so much money, that he did not pay them more. In the upper part of the building is the adjusting room, where the employees are women. Mr. Guern made Spotted Tail say that the gold and silver were pretty to look at, but that he would rather look at the squaws. From the Mint the party were taken to view the picture, "Sheridan's Ride," and while there the poem on the subject was recited, but the Indians were like Casca coming from Cicero's oration in Greek— it was all Greek to them.

They were next driven to the Union League House and handsomely entertained. After being shown through the various beautifully furnished rooms of the club, they were taken to the reception room, where Signor Blitz, who was present, performed some of his most brilliant feats, for their benefit. Spotted Tail was taken in hand to assist in one of the slight-of-hand tricks. The signor produced a small walking cane, which he requested Spotted Tail to hold firmly with both hands, a short distance from either end. He then asked for a ring from any one in the audience, and, on its being produced, placed it against the cane, covering it with a handkerchief; he then quickly withdrew the handkerchief, and left the ring rapidly revolving upon the cane, greatly to the amazement of Spotted Tail. The Indians were allowed to examine the ring to see if there was any opening or secret spring, but failed to find one, and were completely nonplussed. A number of tricks were performed, with which the Indians were highly pleased, and they pronounced the signor a great medicine man. They also said that they had been bountifully feasted since they left home, but that this was the first amusement they had enjoyed. It was suggested that the signor would make a good Peace Commissioner, his feats of legerdemain having the power to break through the apparent stolidity of the Indians as nothing else had. After a fine collation the party took their departure, the entire affair at the Union League House having been a most agreeable one, which left pleasant and lasting impressions upon the minds of the distinguished savages.

A large crowd collected in front of Independence Hall, and remained until a late hour in the afternoon, in the hope of seeing the Indian chiefs; but Spotted Tail and his friends preferred the seclusion of their rooms to making any more visits.

The inhabitants of the City of Brotherly Love were almost too demonstrative for the comfort of their Indian guests.

CHAPTER XXXII.

VISITS IN NEW YORK—BROADWAY AND CENTRAL PARK—ON
BOARD FRENCH FRIGATE.

AFTER a day spent in the city peopled by the descendants of those who, in their dealings with red men, had said, "We are met on the broad pathway of good faith and good will, so that no advantage is to be taken on either side, but all to be openness, brotherhood and love," the Indians were taken by rail to New York, to be still further impressed with the extent of the white man's country, and the number of its people.

On arrival they were provided for at the Astor House, from whose steps could be heard the rumble and roar of the ceaseless train of vehicles passing over the hard paved streets, and where could be seen the vast throng of pedestrians eagerly pressing onward in an endless stream. Here the Indians could see and gain some knowledge of the number of white men in their Great Father's country. They

were shown views of Broadway, the grandest
street in the world, it is said, with its long un-
dulating perspective, and grand panorama of
human activity and industry. They looked
upon the scene with their usual stoicism. Spotted Tail could not be drawn into any expression
of opinion, but Swift Bear announced his conviction that these were the same people, who
had followed their party from Chicago to Washington, Philadelphia, and now to New York.
He could not tell how they were transported,
but was firm in his belief that they were the
same individuals.

There was some excuse for this strange idea,
for the Indians had been kept busy in viewing
new sights and scenes until they were somewhat dazed. There was a similarity too in the
individuals who gazed upon and jostled them
whenever they left the cars, and who crowded
the walks when they made their appearance
from the hotel. In every city the young street
Arabs ran alongside of the carriages when the
Indians were out for a drive, and shouted and
yelled, and called the attention of their friends
to the unusual sight in just the same way. The
inhabitants of an Indian village have such
numbers of ponies, anywhere from six to two
dozen to each family, that they are always
ready to move in a body. An hour's time would
suffice to put a number of thousands of them

under way, with their families, household goods and dwellings.

Swift Bear may have thought that the so-called superior white men had superior facilities for moving his towns and dwellings, and that thousands of them could follow a few Indians. Egotism is a dominant characteristic of the savage, and the idea of a fixed and permanent home for a people does not enter into his philosophy.

The military drama "Not Guilty" was being performed at Niblo's, and was a play calculated to interest the Indians in its scenic effects, so they were taken there and were well pleased. The sight of one hundred and fifty soldiers, with regimental band and drum corps, filled their idea of an entertainment. The embarkation of the volunteers for India, and the field of battle during an engagement, were presented with such scenic surroundings as to make effective tableaux, which were fully understood and enjoyed by the red men, but they were as undemonstrative as living creatures could be.

The following Sunday, June 12th, being a delightful summer day, and the streets being comparatively quiet, carriages were procured, and the Indians driven the length of Broadway and Fifth Avenue to Central Park. The park was clothed in its freshest summer dress, leaves and grass and flowers looking their brightest.

The nomads were here presented with a scene of fairy land, the perfection of an ideal landscape, the work of man, which they could compare with their own boundless park, the prairie, dotted with wild flowers, its outlines broken by high buttes and strips of woodland, the work of nature. While viewing the former they could have pleasant dreams of the latter.

Spotted Tail, who was in the carriage with me, was asked to look at a particularly fine view of the city from a high elevation in the park, and was found to be dreaming indeed. The soft cushions of the carriage, and its gentle motion over the smooth roadway, had rocked him to sleep, while I had supposed that he was being fully impressed with the grandeur of the works of white men.

On our return to the hotel Mr. Stetson brought into the room, where the Indians were enjoying their siesta, a toy velocipedist, and set it in motion. The chiefs and warriors were intensely delighted with it, and all enjoyed a hearty laugh over and over again as it was wound up and set going. Spotted Tail expressed a desire to possess such a toy, and was highly delighted when Mr. Stetson presented him with one.

The next day the Indians were invited by Admiral Lafebre to visit the French frigate "Magicienne," lying at anchor off the Battery.

This invitation was accepted. When the party arrived at the Battery they were immediately surrounded by the usual crowd, and only by shoving and pushing did we manage to gain the stairway leading from the Battery to the water. Here the Admiral's cutter was lying, manned by a crew of eight oarsmen, with a young officer in charge. We were quickly seated in the stern sheets, and the men giving way on their oars, were soon rapidly nearing the frigate.

This was an entirely new experience to the Indians, and as the water was a little rough, and rocked the boat as she cut through the waves, propelled by the strong arms of the crew, they held on to the gunwales with their hands, rather nervously, but their faces had the same expression they would have borne had they been crossing the turbid Missouri in one of their own familiar dug-outs, and they must have given to the subjects of a foreign nation who were rowing them, the impression that a ride of this kind was an every-day occurrence to them.

Having arrived alongside the frigate, the visiting party were received by the admiral and his officers, and were shown to the admiral's cabin, where all were hospitably entertained. Mr. Guern was kept busy translating conversations from English into French and French into

Sioux, according to the wants of the company.
After cake and wine, the admiral and his officers conducted the visitors over the ship.   Her
heavy broadside guns were loaded with blank
cartridges, and the Indians were invited to discharge them.   The small arms were exhibited,
including cutlasses, boarding pikes, revolvers
and rifles.   The latter were of the Chassepot
pattern, in use by the French nation, the breech-
loading arrangements of which are quite different from those of the various arms in use in this
country.   The mechanism of this gun was explained to the Indians, and it was loaded and
discharged as rapidly as possible to show its
effectiveness in this respect.   But they were
each possessed of a Winchester Magazine rifle,
which could be loaded and discharged even
more rapidly, and was a better-looking and
better finished arm, so they were not impressed
by the Chassepot.   If the Indian is too untutored to understand the real merit of white
men's industry in building cities and beautify-
ing the landscape, he is thoroughly alive when
he comes in contact with their implements of
warfare, and on every occasion minutely in-
spects their mechanism, and is quick to perceive
any advantages they may possess.   The Sioux
warrior is as well armed as any in the world, as
dexterous in the use of his weapons, and as solicitous in the care of them, which was, per-

haps, one reason why this delegation was visiting on board a French frigate in New York harbor.

After a somewhat lengthy but informal inspection of the frigate, the visitors bade good bye to their pleasant entertainers, and returned to the hotel.

The next visit was to the *Herald* building, where the Indians were shown through the various departments, and the machinery of the press room put in motion for their benefit. This was a marvel and a mystery to the nomads.

I had been delegated to supervise the purchase of some presents for the Indians, the articles to be selected by themselves, but not to exceed a certain amount in total value. For this purpose I took them to a wholesale house on Broadway which dealt in Indian goods, and here they found many things that they coveted. They each selected blankets, beads, paint, umbrellas, fans and dolls. The dolls were for their children, who were not forgotten by their much-traveled fathers, but the umbrellas and fans were for themselves and not for their faithful squaws, as one might suppose. The hewers of wood and drawers of water have no time to loiter under umbrellas or to fan themselves while gossiping, and these articles belong strictly to the male attire. Swift Bear and the

two warriors each indulged in a roll of German
silver plate, which is used by the Indians for
making rude breast-plates and ornaments to
suspend from the neck. It is also used by
some of the warriors for ornamenting the scalp
lock, being made in this case into a series of
graduated circles, the largest about six inches
in diameter and the smallest about two These
circles are fastened together by strips of tanned
skin, and when worn the largest circle is attached to the scalp lock, and the smaller end
trails near the ground. In addition to their
various selections of goods. each Indian was
provided with a trunk in which to pack his new
possessions. The Indians were invited to visit
many places of interest in the city and harbor,
but they were becoming impatient of the delay
in the East, and constantly asked to be taken
back to their friends on the prairie, to once
more enjoy its boundless freedom. The visit
of the delegation to the cities of New York and
Philadelphia had developed an unexpected
kindness on the part of the people towards
these Indians, which indicated that the masses
were in full sympathy with any efficient movement to ameliorate their condition and advance
them on the road to civilization.

CHAPTER XXXIII.

RETURN HOME—STOP IN CHICAGO, PURCHASES OF HORSES AND
CLOTHING—ARRIVAL AT THE AGENCY.

THE Indians having become surfeited with scenes and incidents of Metropolitan life, I believed that it would not add to their stock of information to keep them against their inclinations, and decided to take them home by the most expeditious route.

Accordingly on the evening of June 13th, we left New York, and commenced the journey westward.

In addition to the presents received in New York, the chiefs and warriors had the promise that they should go home on horseback. A promise of this kind is never forgotten by an Indian, and the party were true to their instincts. Before they had been on the road many hours, they reminded me of the promise of Secretary Cox, and began to scrutinize the different horses seen en route, and to advise me as to the kind of animals they wished me to purchase. They showed the effect of associa-

tion with white men, and isolation from their
friends, and the life they led on their native
prairies, by informing me that they wanted to
meet their people, not only mounted on fine
horses with handsome trappings, but also
dressed in complete suits of clothing, so that
their friends could see at a glance how the
Great Father's people dressed and appeared.
This was rather an unexpected request, coming
from those who a few months before had
treated the gift of a large quantity of coats,
pants and hats with marked disdain, and had
intimated that it was far from their intention to
appear before their adherents clothed in such
habliments.

This desire for change of costume seemed an
indication that if these simple-minded people
were brought into more intimate relations with
civilization, and were surrounded by a pre-
ponderance of the white race in their daily life,
a change of dress and habits would soon be
realized, and their hold upon savage life would
be loosened.

We made our first halt in Chicago, where
I informed the Indians I could purchase their
horses to better advantage than at any point
farther west, but that they would have to follow after us in freight cars, and that it would
be some days before they would be received.
The Indians displayed their usual childish im-

patience by not wanting any delay of the kind,
So the horses were not purchased, but the
Indians selected their saddles and bridles,
which they were privileged to carry with them
as baggage.

Having plenty of spare time they were shown
about the city, being taken as usual in carriages.   While viewing the different points of
interest they exhibited their knowledge of the
world and their new-made ideas by commenting upon the buildings and parks, and compar-
ing them with those they had lately seen in the
East.   In driving about the city we came
to one of the tunnels running under the river.
When it was explained to the Indians that they
were about to ride under the water, they not
only exhibited much interest in the work, but
flatly refused to pass through the tunnel.
The street running through dipped down at
such a curve that they could not see their way
through, and they peered suspiciously into the
opening and concluded it was not safe.   It was
something unheard of to ride under a river, and
there might be some hidden danger.   I reminded them that my chances of injury were
the same as theirs, and, finally, with the top of
the carriage thrown back, that they might better see all that was going on about them, they
consented to drive through.   But they did not
like it, and were evidently relieved when it was

over. They had often passed through the
dangers of battle, and would willingly do so
again, but an unknown and unseen danger required moral courage, which is not possessed
by savages.

Twenty-four hours of railroading brought us
to Sioux City, where the Indians began to feel
more at home. On the streets could be seen a
stray Winnebago, on leave from his reservation in Nebraska, the well-known half-breed,
and familiar ranchman; while tied to the banks
of the turbulent Missouri was the not unusual
stern-wheel steamboat, which brought their
supplies to the agency. They threw off some
of their reserve, and conversed more freely with
those about them.

Here the horses were to be purchased, and
the market was inspected for suitable ones; not
ponies, but American horses—a name applied
in the West to the ordinary horse in use
among white men. The dealers in these useful
animals were soon aware that four were wanted,
and a perceptible rise in the market was noticed. The usual trials of the gait and speed of
the horses were undertaken, and quite an
amount of time consumed in dickering over
the prices to be paid, but finally differences
were adjusted and the Indians supplied with
their coveted horses, upon which they intended
to appear before their friends at home. A full

suit of clothing was bought for each Indian, and taken to the hotel. In the seclusion of their rooms they donned the dress of white men, but could not make up their minds to appear in public. They were already too far west for the change, so the suits were packed in the trunks among the other novelties. The party submitted to the blandishments of a photographer whom they had seen up the river, and consented to sit for their pictures, which was a great departure for them. Spotted Tail, however, would not look at the object-glass of the camera during the sitting, as therein was hidden the bad medicine. The old question had to be settled, whether to embark on a steamboat or take an overland conveyance. Spotted Tail had heard rumors of the sickness of his favorite wife in the Brulé camp, and he was anxious to make the balance of the journey as quickly as possible, so recourse was had to private conveyances, and a day's journey brought us to Yankton. The newly-purchased horses had their first treatment at the hands of Indians, and, being led behind our vehicles, the sixty-four mile journey reduced their spirited antics of the morning.

The Indians were now a little less than a hundred miles from their homes and friends, and expressed all the eagerness of children to press forward to their destination. The ride from Yankton to Whetstone Agency was over the familiar prairie that abounds in Dakota. The distance was so great that we had to halt for the night *en route* at a lone ranch, which furnished the substantial meals of the locality, and that was about all. The mosquito season was at its height, and there was no rest for man or beast. Mosquito bars were not furnished by our host, so that sleep under the mud roof was impossible. The Indians covered themselves completely with their blankets and bivouacked for the night, apparently enjoying an undisturbed slumber; but the white men vainly contended against the assaults of myriads of full-grown vigorous mosquitoes, who increase in strength, activity and biting powers as you journey towards the north. We found that it required some experience to cover oneself completely, head and foot, with a blanket of a hot night and still sleep. The mosquitoes attacked our animals so vigorously that smudges had to be started, the smoke from which relieved them of some of their tormentors and kept them from breaking away from their tethers.

Not finding rest at the ranch it was left behind at break of day. A short stop was made at Yankton Agency, where the chief of the Yanktons, "Strike-the-ree," had an opportunity of interviewing Spotted Tail and

learning the result of his mission.   At Fort
Randall Spotted Tail heard of the death of
his favorite wife, which dampened what otherwise proved to be a pleasant ending of a long
journey.   The grand éntree of the chiefs and
warriors, mounted and newly clad in white
men's dress, was abandoned.   When the party
arrived at the agency, Swift Bear, Yellow Hair
and Fast Bear disappeared among their friends,
while Spotted Tail journeyed alone to his camp
in sadness and sorrow.   He gave away his fine
new horse, saddle and bridle, his beaded
blanket, leggins and moccasins, while his well-
packed trunk, filled with presents, was also
"thrown upon the prairie," as the Indians say,
in the abandonment of his overwhelming grief.

   The chiefs and warriors never appeared in
their suits of clothing.   The predominance of
Indian modes and customs had restored their
ideas of dress to their normal condition, and
they were all once more Indians among Indians.

CHAPTER XXXIV.

AFFAIRS AT THE AGENCY — DIFFICULTY IN SUPPRESSING
WHISKEY TRAFFIC—VISIT FROM WM. WELSH—FIRE THUN-
DER—CHANGE OF AGENCY.

UPON returning to the agency after an
absence of over a month in the East with
the visiting delegation, about the same state of
affairs existed as before. The garrison of
troops had shelter for themselves, made from
rough sawed logs, and had built block houses
of the same material at opposite angles of a
stockade, inclosing the new buildings, thus
making a defensive retreat in case of an outbreak among the wards of the Government.
This gave a sense of security not before enjoyed to such employees of the Government as
were obliged to remain in contact with the
Indians.

The season had advanced, and the results of
the cultivation of the soil were visible. The
beetle had destroyed the potato vines, but the
grasshoppers had spared the corn. The white-
men with Indian wives had been reasonably

industrious, and fair crops were the result of their labor. At the same time they had by their example and influence given a lesson in agriculture to their brothers-in-law and other Indian relatives, which would have been of great importance had the latter shown the least desire to be instructed, but it was entirely thrown away, and the squaws were still the husbandmen.

About this time Mr. William Welsh, of Philadelphia, a practical philanthropist, came to the agency on a visit. He had an earnest desire to elevate the material and spiritual condition of the Indians. His plan was to come among them, and by making himself familiar with their actual condition, to be able to suggest to the authorities such means as he thought best to accomplish the good sought. Spotted Tail, Swift Bear, and the warriors who had met Mr. Welsh at Philadelphia, greeted their benefactor with more than ordinary heartiness, and in their primitive way made an effort to entertain him.

In the Council that was held the various chiefs and headmen represented to Mr. Welsh the evil effects produced by the introduction of intoxicating liquors among their friends, and pictured with eloquence scenes in their quiet lives when they were away from its baneful influence, and from association with such white men as brought it among them. In this connection a circumstance occurred which illustrates the difficulty of controlling this class of men.

The land situated on the left bank of the Missouri river was known as Ceded land, and there was no law to prevent a squatter settling upon it, and requiring a title when it should be for entry or sale by the Government. If the original occupant could not thus obtain an immediate title, he had by possession a recognized claim, which his friends and neighbors respected. To "jump" such a claim might bring into use the shotgun and rifle; the sympathy of the community being always on the side of the original occupant; so under the primitive law of the locality a man staked out his claim and built his log hut without fear of being dispossessed, taking care while doing so to have his claim conform to the legal sub-divisions of land known as "forties" and "eighties."

A squatter had established himself opposite the agency on three "forties," which made a tract of land a quarter of a mile deep and three-quarters long, lying immediately on the river bank. Here he built a ranch on a prominent point overlooking the agency grounds, and soon became notorious in the neighborhood as the principal vendor of villainous whiskey, a bold, unscrupulous man, who by his secret traffic accumulated a good deal of the currency in circulation about the agency. The chiefs denounced this man, and wanted him removed. Mr. Welsh promised to have it done, and as he could not invoke the law, did the next best thing, and very generously bought the log cabin, and the shadow of title held by the ranchman on the three "forties," exacting, as part of the bargain, a pledge from the man that he would leave the country. This was all very well, and apparently a good bargain, ridding the Indians of a mischievous enemy.

But soon after Mr. Welsh's departure for the East, the ranchman returned with a wagon load of whiskey, staked out a new claim of three "forties," next to those which he had sold, and put up a ranch, which was quite as convenient for his business as the first one. After fully establishing himself, he sent word to the agency that he would like to sell out again, and as it was reported that he had received twelve hundred dollars from Mr Welsh for his former ranch and claim, he could for once be believed, and he had no takers.

During Mr. Welsh's visit a large quantity of annuity goods were received, and he inspected the quality and quantity of the goods, and witnessed their distribution. In a council he spoke at considerable length of the efforts being made to procure, from this time on, the best of blankets and provisions for the use of the Indians, and his remarks met with constant expressions of approbation and approval from his hearers ; but when he went on to tell of his great desire to establish schools and churches among them, and to have them become Christians, I was constrained to notice that his eloquence elicited no " hows," and was listened to with the most stolid indifference by those whom he wished to benefit. In the course of his remarks Mr. Welsh spoke of having lately seen the President in Washington, and in telling them of the latter's interest in listening to plans to send them the best of supplies, and ministers and teachers for them and their children, he said that he had the ear of the Great Father, who listened to his words spoken for them. Fire Thunder was present, but had not received any particular amount of attention, and being opposed to the making of any permanent improvements at the agency, and to changing his nomadic life, he was inclined to find fault if possible. Accordingly when every one was through talking, he announced that he had something to say to Mr. Welsh. He commenced by asking the latter if he really intended to send out better blankets and beef cattle, and to build churches and school houses for the Indians. Mr. Welsh replied that he

certainly did.   Then Fire Thunder wished to
know if he had the Great Father's ear, as he
had said.   Again Mr. Welsh answered in the
affirmative.   "Then," said Fire Thunder, "if
you have the Great Father's ear, let's see it!"
In vain Mr. Welsh tried to explain that it was
only a figure of speech.   Fire Thunder having
announced to the Indians that Mr. Welsh was
a liar, and like all white men made a great
many promises but did not fulfill them, drew
his blanket about him, and stalked out of the
council room.

Through the instrumentality of Mr. Welsh,
church service was held at the agency for the
first time in its history, one end of a partially
filled store house doing duty as chapel.   He
also succeeded in establishing a school and
having a teacher appointed, thus fulfilling immediately his promise to the Indians, and giving them proof of his earnest desire to place
before them instrumentalities for gaining knowledge of a better life.

Mr. Welsh remained at the agency for a
number of days, and was much impressed with
the primitive life of the Indians, and the great
work to be accomplished to bring them to realize that they must abandon their present savage
life for that civilized life offered by white men.
He left the agency with the best wishes of all
for the success of his philanthropic plans.

General D. S. Stanley, of the army, also visited the agency. He commanded the military district within whose boundary were located the Sioux Indians of Dakota, both those who were fed and clothed at the agencies upon the Missouri River and those who still proclaimed their hostility, and remained at a distance in camps on the tributaries of the Yellowstone River. The General was well known among the Sioux, both friendly and hostile, and held in good esteem by them. It was the common report on the river that he never turned a deaf ear toward an Indian when seeking counsel, nor allowed him to depart from his door when needy, without some substantial gift of food or clothing.

This contributed to mutual good will, which was productive of substantial benefit in his dealings with these people.

Spotted Tail having recovered from the effects of the loss of his favorite wife, began to recall the promises made to him while at Washington, and to make inquiries as to the time when he should be allowed to select the location for an agency on White River. It was understood that this was not purely a movement of Spotted Tail and his people, or of the Indians at the agency, but that the whites and half-breeds at the latter place were interested in having the change accomplished, as it would involve having all the supplies transported overland from the Missouri River about a hundred and fifty miles, and about the same distance from the Union Pacific Railroad. Of course this would have to be paid for by the Government, at a cost of many thousands of dollars every year. There was a ring formed to reap the benefit of this outlay, and, strange to say, it was outside of Washington influences, although connected with Indian affairs. There was also a desire on the part of the whites associated with the Indians to work their way toward the comparatively unknown El Dorado supposed to be in the vicinity of the Black Hills.

The matter of locating the new agency, and the plans for its accomplishment, had to go through the Department and its immediate channels for approval—a difficult route to navigate, requiring much time.

CHAPTER XXXV.

SIOUX INDIANS AS HISTORIANS—HUNTING ON THE REPUBLI-
CAN IN KANSAS—NUMBER OF BEEF CATTLE ON HAND—
WOLF HUNT OF MEDICINE MEN.

THE Sioux Indians do not possess knowledge that enables them to make lasting records of events. They erect no monuments, neither transcribe upon paper, plate or parchment, episodes in their existence that can be deciphered by succeeding generations. Their rude hieroglyphics painted upon buffalo robes, rocks or tepees, may recall some idea of the succession of events in the history of some individual or band belonging to a tribe; but as a record to be translated by others than the actors or their cotemporaries they are of no use. So far as I was able to understand, their only history was in the legends passed from one to another. It was one of their favorite pastimes to recount these inauthentic narratives, and groups of the men would often be seen, one leading in the recountal of some daring deed of an individual or of some en-

counter with their hereditary enemies the
Pawnees or Crows, the others listening with
many marks of interest and even excitement ;
for among themselves the Sioux are far from
stoical or undemonstrative.   Incidents recounted in this way soon become changed, and
the narrators tell the wildest and most improb-
able stories with little or no intention of exag-
geration.   It was something in this way that
Spotted Tail, upon his return from Washington, created a false impression upon his listen-
ers on at least one subject.   He had kept no
record of events during a long journey
crowded with strange scenes and incidents,
and he had spoken so often while in Washington on the subject of his people being allowed
to leave their reservation to hunt buffalo on
the Republican, that it is not to be wondered
at that he finally came to believe that his request had been granted, while in truth no
direct reply had been given.   It was on this
subject that he was most eagerly questioned
on his return, and it was the theme of many
councils.   Finding that there was a strong
impression that permission had been given, I
referred the subject to Washington, and an
official denial in writing at last put an end to
the question,

Soon after my return from the East, a change
was made in the manner of purchasing supplies

for the daily food of the Indians, the business being again placed under the control of the same department that administered upon their affairs. This largely increased the responsibilities of the agent, and gave him abundant opportunity for the display of executive ability. Heretofore the stores had been under the control of an officer, who was not only responsible to the Commissary Department of the Army, but, in addition, had the verification of the quantity of the articles which arrived at the agency, and was required to see that they were properly stored. He then issued them from time to time as called upon by the agent. Under the regime of the Commissary Department. the beef cattle had been kept by the contractor until wanted, the commissary officer receiving only such number as would be required to fill the orders of the agent for the time being, thereby placing the cost and risk of maintenance upon the contractor, and dividing the accountability between the commissary officer and the agent. But there are different modes of transacting public business, and any comparisons might be invidious.

The Indians could not hunt buffalo, but they could feast their eyes upon a herd of two thousand head of broad-horned cattle that dotted the prairie hard by their habitations, and gave promise of an abundance of food.

Under orders I had received this number, and
of course had to account for them ; also to see
that they were properly herded and kept on
good grazing ground ; that their valuable flesh,
bought and paid for by the Government, should
not be lessened from lack of proper sustenance
before they were issued and consumed by the
Indians.   It was one thing to receive fat cattle
and another to keep them so for months upon
the prairie grass of Dakota, commencing in
July, when the hot winds and scorching sun
had destroyed much of the vegetation.   The
large herd had to be divided into at least three,
with a corps of herders with each, and kept
from twenty to thirty miles away from the
agency, for the Indians had on hand nearly
fifteen hundred ponies, who consumed all the
grass in the vicinity   Frequent visits were
necessary to inspect the different herds, to
verify their numbers, and to watch a not over-
scrupulous set who would not guard the interests of the Government any too faithfully with
the best overseeing.   Then, too, there were
stories afloat in the buoyant atmosphere which
surrounds an Indian agency that these cattle,
having been received at Whetstone, were to be
driven to other agencies to be receipted for
again, which was by no means a physical impossibility, and altogether a more probable
proceeding than many of the dishonest tricks

charged to those who have the fortune to be
agents for the ubiquitous Indians.

An Episcopal minister from Sioux City, who
was spending a part of his summer vacation at
the agency, enjoying the wild life and the
removal from every-day scenes, accompanied
me on one of my inspecting tours, together
with the physician at the agency. We had a
delightful ride over the prairie in the direction
of Ponca Creek, along whose banks was the
best of pasturage, and whose waters furnished
the coolest of draughts. It was late in the day
before the object of our visit was accomplished,
and we had to camp for the night and partake
of a herder's meal. The latter consisted of
"jerked beef," cooked by placing a piece of
it upon the end of a stick, and holding it near
a camp fire until roasted, a slice of bacon prepared in the same way, coffee and hard biscuit,
and altogether made a delightful repast,
relished after a ride of thirty miles in the
pure bracing air of the prairie.

After the siesta and smoke in the twilight,
by the flickering light of the camp fire, enliv-
ened by song and story, we retired to our tent,
spread our blankets, and were soon soundly
sleeping. About midnight my two friends were
aroused from their slumber by the noise unusual to them, of the crying of a pack of wolves,
who had taken position on the opposite bank

of the creek, and who barked and howled their lamentations to such an extent as to dispel all sleep for the time. Finding that their unearthly noises did not drive us away, they finally retired, but not so my guests. There was no more sleep for them, and they spent the remainder of the night in listening to every slight noise without our tent, imagining it was the approach of a stealthy wolf. At last they were sure that they heard one dragging his tail through the tall grass. The two doctors peered into the darkness, through a crack in the door of the tent, one above the other, each with rifle ready. Nearer and nearer came the skulking animal. By a whispered conference, it was agreed that they should fire together at a given signal. About this time I roused up, and, seeing them on the watch, inquired the cause of their unusual excitement. They told me to listen to the wolf dragging his tail in the grass near at hand. I boldly announced that wolves did not drag their tails, and suggested that it might be one of our horses, who had gotten loose, and was dragging his lariat. A more careful reconnoitre proved this to be the case. My interference came none too soon, for in another minute the two medicine men would have buried the contents of their rifles in the side of one of our best horses.

On our return to the agency next day,

they shared the honors of their wolf hunt.
In due time the final arrangements were completed for the movement of the Indians to their
new agency on White River, and the first provisions, including cattle, were forwarded to that
point, which was to be designated for the time
being their permanent home.

The Indians entered upon the new movement
with apparent delight, their instincts leading
them always in the direction of change. Old
hearth-stones or familiar scenes, with hallowed
memories, do not enter into their ken, and a
home permanently located has no charm for
them. Any spot on the broad prairie, which
will supply a few natural wants, will be made
in an hour or two their local habitation. So,
still clinging to their nomadic habits, they followed, with alacrity, after the new base of supplies. The bottom lands of White River and
its tributaries possessed no more arable land
than those of Whetstone Creek and the Missouri; but the cultivation of the soil, with all
the inducements offered, was only a matter to
be discussed in council, and kept an open question, to be again and again resorted to as a pos
sible future contingency.

They had been abundantly supplied with excellent food and a reasonable amount of clothing, but they were not satisfied. Conciliatory
measures dominating among those in authority,

a change was considered necessary, regardless of cost, and their wishes were gratified.

The chiefs and warriors who had been favored with an opportunity of seeing the works of white men were not zealous in expatiating upon the wonders seen in the East. I think they refrained from telling their experience, fearing that they would lose caste among their less enlightened associates—a result predicted by Spotted Tail. Their visit was never referred to except incidentally, and then only in connection with some promise that had been made.

Nevertheless, it was a little of the leaven, which might eventually leaven the whole lump.

CHAPTER XXXVI.

LEAVE THE SIOUX AFTER EIGHTEEN MONTHS' INTERCOURSE—
SOME REFLECTIONS ON THE INDIAN QUESTION.

IN December, 1870, I took leave of the Sioux Indians, and returned to my usual duties. In the eighteen months' of my intercourse with them, I had seen many things to make my association far from disagreeable. Their simple form of government, their picturesque dress and habitations, their patriarchal surroundings, their hospitality, the bravery and endur-ance of the men, and the virtue and faithfulness of the women, were to be admired.

I had seen them in their villages, removed from disturbing influences, living in quiet and peaceful contentment. They were easily persuaded and governed.

But a disturbing element as old as the discovery of the continent, was at hand. The white man, a representative of a superior race, armed with greater knowledge, created discontent and brought confusion into their councils, and made the administration of Indian affairs

an unsatisfactory work from which I was glad
to escape. The superior race, moved by an un-
controlled and restless spirit of enterprise, will
carry civilization and its accompaniments
throughout the extent of our country, and in
its rapid progress, ever encroaches ruthlessly
upon the domains of the Indians, in spite of
treaties and promised protection. Policies are
inaugurated and pursued according to the dic-
tates of the ruling sentiment of the hour. The
philanthropist with Utopian ideas, would have
the Indian secluded from contact with the
pioneer, who is engaged in planting the seeds of
future civilization near the Indians' possessions, and the pioneer finding the latter a troublesome neighbor, cumbering the ground, would
have him exterminated ; while the spirit of fair
play, dominant in the Anglo-Saxon race, suggests means to ameliorate the asperities incident to the inevitable conflict, various views are
advocated, and the results of wide discussion
are crystalized into laws, the application of
which make the actual plan followed in dealing with the Indians, who being the weaker
party must accept the consequences if remaining within their jurisdiction. The Sioux are
still a no contemptible power, and when further
encroachments shall compel them to act, have
the means to save their customs and mode of
life from the inexorable fate which will over-

take the weaker tribes. The strong and active are not likely to surrender their cherished habits without a struggle, after which they may fold their tepees, and journeying over well known trails, join their friends and relations across our northern boundary, and find a new hunting park in a not unfamiliar land, where the encroachments of the settler do not make such rapid strides, and a fixed policy secures the fulfillment of all promises made.

The various duties and responsibilities of the Indian agent, doing duty in the far west, have been touched upon in this narrative. Without the boundaries of civilization, isolated from the associations and comforts of a home, pestered and tormented by some of the worst specimens of white humanity, seeing the credulity of the Indians imposed upon, and the good effects of honorable dealing neutralized, often traduced and villified by men whom he may have thwarted in some nefarious scheme, made to share the consequences of deficiency in supplies over which he never had control, and made responsible by the public for any outbreak among the untamed and tantalized savages under his charge, his lines are not cast in pleasant places.

It has come to be believed that association with the Indian leads to dishonesty. On the contrary, I believe the tendency is the other way; the simple confidence which the Indian places in his agent, makes the latter his protector, and, unless a very depraved character, he will naturally guard him and his rights.

The theoretical rules for the transaction of the affairs of the Indians are one thing, and the practical application of the rules when mingling with them in the every day discharge of duty. is another.   Usually the Indian agent comes in contact with his duties perfectly unprepared by experience.   He has a few lines of vague generalities about the beneficence of the Government, and a book of regulations containing the theoretical rules for his guidance.   With these he is expected to cope with difficulties and effect grand improvements.

The amount of money annually expended at each of the large agencies in the West, would in the ordinary affairs of life demand ability in the agent, which would have a market value of at least three-fold the amount now allowed by law to an Indian agent.   Any mercantile house in the East, having a branch in some isolated locality in the far West, which transacted a business amounting to half a million of dollars a year, would see to it that they not only had an experienced and competent agent, but that he was fully compensated for the trials and vicissitudes incident to his location and the duties which he performed.   He would be often visited, his accounts scrutinized, and his duties supervised. He would be encouraged in the direction of making him a good and faithful representative of his employers, and would be assured of reward for faithful service done.

The reverse of this usually awaits the Indian agent; he is occasionally visited by parties following the scent of some supposed rascality, but left to himself and his labors, if he escapes the usual charge of dishonesty; and his faithful service is more than likely to be rewarded by summary dismissal to make place for his successor.

According to the laws of compensation, the Indian agent is about what he is made by his employers, and the latter obtain what they bargain for. Therefore, it is reasonable to believe that a more intimate acquaintance with the actual condition of affairs among the Indians, by those who control the actions of the agent in their midst, and a more thorough system of accountability, an increased salary, and longer term of office for the agent, with some surety of reward for faithful service, would be of immense gain, and would take but a moiety from the millions of dollars annually expended by a beneficent Government upon the Indians of the plains.

APPENDIX.

REPORT OF BREVET-MAJOR GENERAL D. S. STANLEY, U. S. A.

HEADQUARTERS, MIDDLE DISTRICT,
FORT SULLY, D. T.,
August, 20, 1869.

General:

I have the honor to report the following as the Indian tribes and bands in this district with approximate numbers of each, and nearest military post or agency to which the several bands resort; also their division into hostile and peaceable:

1. Gros Ventres, Mandans, and Rees, two thousand; Fort Stevenson and Berthold. Peaceable.

2. Upper Yanctonais, three thousand; Forts Rice and Grand River; range to Yellowstone. Mostly peaceable.

3. Oncpapas, two thousand; Forts Rice and

Grand River. Fifteen hundred hostile; five hundred peaceable.

4. Blackfeet Sioux, nine hundred ; Grand River. Two hundred hostile ; seven hundred peaceable.

5. Two Kettles, fifteen hundred ; Forts Sully and Thompson. Five hundred hostile ; one thousand peaceable.

6. Sans Arcs, fifteen hundred ; Fort Sully. One thousand hostile; five hundred peaceable.

7. Minneconjoux, two thousand; Forts Sully and Grand River. Sixteen hundred hostile; four hundred peaceable.

8. Upper Brulés, fifteen hundred ; Fort Sully and White River. Eight hundred hostile ; seven hundred peaceable.

9. Lower Yanctonais, one thousand ; Fort Thompson. Peaceable.

10. Brulés of the Platte, fifteen hundred; Whetstone. Supposed peaceable.

11. Ogallalas, two thousand; Whetstone. Fifteen hundred hostile ; five hundred peaceable.

12. Yanctons, twenty-five hundred; Fort Randall. Peaceable.

The Gros Ventres, Mandans, and Rees are well behaved, and give no trouble. They are at war with the friendly Sioux, but have peace with the hostile Oncpapas and Minneconjoux, and carry on a trade with them.

The Upper Yanctonais, ruled by the chiefs "Two Bears" and "Black Eyes," are perhaps the best behaved Indians on the river.

The Oncpapas are turbulent and mischievous. Those who pretend to be friendly live at Grand River reservation, but give so much trouble that it is doubtful whether the agency can be kept on that side. Their chief is "Bear Rib."

The Blackfeet Sioux are quiet and well behaved. Their principal chief is "The Grass."

The Two Kettles, Sans Arcs and Minneconjoux draw rations at Cheyenne. The first two are quiet; the Minneconjoux are turbulent and very insolent. The chief of the Two Kettles is the "Tall Mandan;" of the Sans Arcs, "Burnt Face;" of the Minneconjoux, the "Iron Horn" and "Little White Swan."

The Lower Brulés have a reservation and cultivate at White River; draw rations at Fort Thompson. They acknowledge no chief; are perfect Ishmaelites, wandering in small bands thousands of miles over the prairies; are treacherous beyond all other Sioux, and commit most of the rascalities which occur in this district.

The Lower Yanctonais are peaceable, and are trying to farm at Fort Thompson.

The Brulés of the Platte generally stay from twenty to one hundred miles out from Whetstone, coming into that place for their provisions. Their disposition is very suspicious, and, like their brethren, the Upper Brulés, are not to be trusted.

The Ogallalas, at Whetstone, are well behaved.

At the agencies established for the Sioux, there is one class of Indians which has been friendly for four or five years, and are nearly permanent residents, only leaving from time to time to hunt or pick wild fruit. With this class there is no trouble. There is another class passing half their time at these agencies and half in the hostile camps. They abuse the agents, threaten their lives, kill their cattle at night, and do anything they can to oppose the civilizing movement, but eat all the provisions they can get, and thus far have taken no lives.

If the agencies were removed east of the Missouri we could suppress these violent and troublesome fellows. The hostiles have representatives from every band ; but the leading band in hostility is the Oncpapas.

During the winter for the past two years, almost the entire hostile Sioux have camped together in one big camp on the Rosebud, near the Yellowstone. In the summer time they break up and spread over the prairies either to hunt, plunder, or come into the posts to beg.

I am, very respectfully,

Your obedient servant,

D. S. STANLEY,
Col. 22d Infantry, Bvt. Maj. Gen.

Bvt. Brig'r General O. D. GREENE, U.S.A.,
Asst. Adjt. Gen. Dept. of Dakota.

INDEX